•Bartholomew

MINI
BRITAIN

Bartholomew

A Division of HarperCollins*Publishers*

Bartholomew
A Division of HarperCollins Publishers
Duncan Street
Edinburgh
EH9 1TA

First published 1987
Revised Edition 1990, 1991, 1992

Copyright © Bartholomew 1987, 1990, 1991, 1992

ISBN 0 7028 1874 7 (Paperback)
ISBN 0 7028 1966 2 (Deluxe Hardback)

Printed in Great Britain
by Bartholomew, HarperCollins
Manufacturing, Edinburgh

The contents of this edition of the Mini Atlas Britain are believed
correct at the time of printing. Nevertheless, the publisher can
accept no responsibility for errors or omissions, or changes in
the detail given.

E/B 5229

CONTENTS

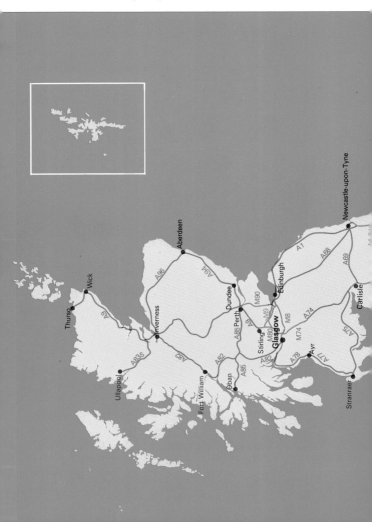

Page 103-104   **KEY**   Page 1-102

	motorway	Junction — Service Area — Restricted Access Junction, under construction
	dual carriageway	
	primary route	A11
	other "A" roads	A529
	"B" road	B1010
	unclassified road	
	narrow road with passing places	
	distance in miles	6 31
	gradient: viewpoint	
— — F — —	car ferry	
✈	airport	
	scenic area	
	built up area	
	place of popular interest	*
	sandy beach	
	sailing centre	
	motor racing circuit	
	race course	
	golf course	
	youth hostel	▲
	chairlift	
	spot height (feet)	3187
	national boundary	

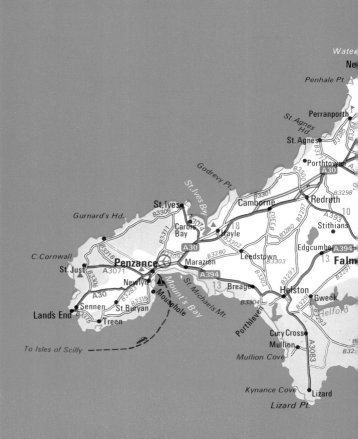

Bude
Stratton
A3072
Orridge
A3012
Oxent
Holsworthy
Highampton
Hatherleigh
Exbourne
Widemouth Bay
Tamar
A388
A3079
A386
B3215
ak
Whitstone
Clawton
Okehampton
S.Z
A39
A386
Whic
B3263
A3079
30
Ottery
Wolf
Bridestowe
Sourton
A386
19
Davidstow
Piperspool
Lifton
A30
B3278
Downtown
amelford
A395
Launceston
Lydford
DARTMOOR
16
Fivelanes
S. Petherwin
Milton Abbot
Dart
A30
Postbridge
Bolventor
776
B3257
A388
B3362
Tavy
For
Bodmin
Merrivale Br
B3357
1252
Moor
892
Upton Cross
Kellybray
Tavistock
Princetown
Two Bridges
703
Fowey
B3254
A327
A390
Gunnislake
B3212
1100
13
St.Ive
18
Callington
B3212
Yelverton
8
Dobwalls
Liskeard
Bere Alston
15
Plym
A390
Tideford
A388
Erme
20
W.Taphouse
A386
Cornwood
S.
ostwithiel
B3359
B3254
B3252
St.Germans
B3249
Saltash
Toll
PLYMOUTH
Pelynt
Polbathic
Torpoint
Plympton
A38
Rybr
W.Looe
E.Looe
A374
Devonport
A379
B3211
ey
A387
St.George's I.
B3247
Yealmpton
Modbury
A399
Polperro
Whitsand Bay
Yealm
B3186
bin Hd.
Rame Hd.
Plymouth Sound
Newton Ferrers
Stoke Pt.
Bigbury on Sea
Bigbury Bay
Ma
Bolt Tail

To Santander
To Roscoff

Lundy

Ilfraco
Bull Pt.
Mortehoe
Woolacombe B3343
Morte Bay
Baggy Pt.
Saunton

Barnstaple or
Bideford Bay

Appledore

ns
A

B3236

Hartland Pt.
Clovelly
Hartland Quay
Hartland
Horns Cross
Ford
Monkleigh
B3248
26
A39
Stibb Cross
B3227

Sharpnose
Petrocks
Torridge
Kilkhampton
B3254
Bude
Stratton
A3072
Holsworthy
Highampton
*Widemouth
Bay*
A388
A3079
Cambeak
Tamar
Clawton
A39
Whitstone
Wolf
Boscastle
B3263
Tintagel Hd.
30
Ottery
Brides
Tintagel
19
B3254
Port Isaac
B3263
Davidstow
Lifton
A30
Piperspool
Launceston
Lyd
Camelford
A395
Camel
Fivelanes
Milton Abbot
Polzeath
B3314
A30
S.
Petherwin
A388
B2257
St. Kew
Highway
Bolventor
776
B3239

B3267
Clovelly
B3237
Stibb Cross

Bideford

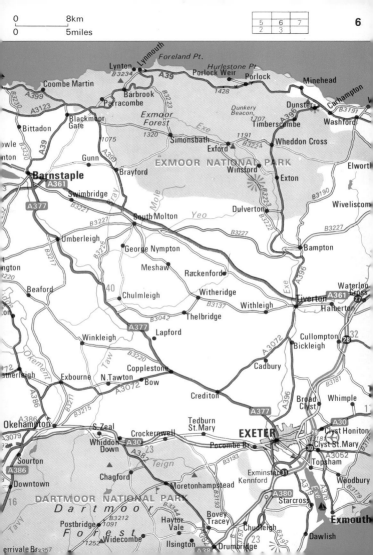

9

nine miles to one inch

Warminster
Heytesbury
Shrewton
B3086
Bulford
A303
Wherwe

B3095
Longbridge Deverill 21
Winterbourne
B3087 Stoke
Amesbury
Cholderton
A343
A3057
Middle Wallop
Stockbridge

A350
Deptford
A303
Stapleford
Lopcombe
Corner
A338

Chicklade
Wylye
A36
A345
A30
Test

en ey
59
Barford
A360
K
S

E.Knoyle
Hindon *B3089*
Wilton
A3094
Salisbury
A3057

28
Fovant
Dunbridge

gham
Shaftesbury
Broad
Chalke
A354
Coombe
Bissett
A36
Whiteparish
Romsey 29
Rownha
3

081
42
Downton
A27
23

ur
Sixpenny
Handley
23
Woodyates
A338
B3080
Landford
B3078
Ower
Cadnam
M27
A36
M2

ston
Fontmell
Magna
B3081
18
Godshill
Stoney Cross
A336
Totton

ster Newton
A350
Cashmoor Corner
B3078
Fordingbridge
19
A31
SOUTHAMP

Stourpaine
Tarrant
Hinton
Cranborne
Verwood
Ibsley
Lyndhurst
A35

on
A354
Horton
Avon
New Forest

d Forum
B3082
B3072
B3081
Ringwood
NEW FOREST
B3056

B3075
West Moors
Brockenhurst
Beaulie

7
14
Wimborne Minster
A31
Ferndown
10
St. Leonards
B3347
B3055

orne rew
Almer
A31
22
A348
Fricketts Cross
12
B3058
Boldre

Bere Regis
Morden
A350
Kinson
Sopley
B3055
Lymingto

28
Lytchett Minster
A35
A3049
Winton
Hinton
Milton
A337
Downton
B3058

Wool ghton
A351
Longfleet
Boscombe
Christchurch
Christchurch Bay

E.Lulworth
Downs
Poole
BOURNEMOUTH
Yar

Kingston
Corfe
Castle
Poole Harb.
Totland
B3

Wareham
A352
Studland
Alum Bay
Freshwater
Bay

B3351
Swanage
The Needles
Freshwater Bay

B3069
Durlston Hd.
To Cherbourg

St. Albans Hd.
To Cherbourg
(summer only)
& Channel Is.

0   8km

0   5miles

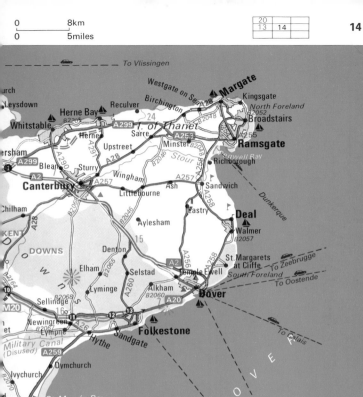

– – – – – 🚢 – – – – – To Vlissingen

ırch
Leysdown
Herne Bay
Whitstable
B2205
Herne
ersham
A299
Blean
Sturry
Chilham
Canterbury
A2
A257
KENT
A28
DOWNS
Denton
Elham
B2065
10
B2068
Sellindge
Lyminge
M20
Newingreen
B2067
16
11
12
13
et
Lympne
A26
Military Canal
(Disused)
A259
Ivychurch
B2070
omney
Littlestone-on-Sea
B2075
d
Greatstone-on-Sea
Dungeness

Reculver
Westgate on Sea
A28
Birchington
B2048
A299
T. of Thanet
Sarre
A253
Upstreet
Minster
A28
B2046
Stour
Wingham
Littlebourne
Ash
Aylesham
Eastry
B2046
A257
A256
Richborough
Sandwich
A258
A2
Selstad
Alkham
B2060
A260
Temple Ewell
St.Margarets
at Cliffe
South Foreland
A258
Dover
A20
Folkestone
Sandgate
Hythe
St Mary's Bay

Margate
Kingsgate
North Foreland
2052
Broadstairs
A255
Ramsgate
Sarwell Bay
Dunkerque
Deal
Walmer
B2057

🚢 To Zeebrugge
🚢 To Oostende

🚢 To Calais

🚢 To Boulogne
🚢 To Boulogne

S T R A I T   O F   D O V E R

0 ____ 8km
0 ____ 5miles

Stone
Stoke Mandeville
A4129
Wendover
Princes Risborough
Gt. Missenden
Chinnor
Stokenchurch
W. Wycombe
High Wycombe
Lane End
Stonor
Marlow
Cookham
Maidenhead
Wargrave
Twyford
Sonning
Wokingham
Bracknell
Easthampstead
Crowthorne
Bagshot
Eversley
Camberley
Blackwater
Hartley Wintney
Fleet
Odiham
Aldershot
Farnborough
Farnham
Guildford
Godalming
Milford
Hascombe
Dunsfold
Kingsley
Hindhead
Chiddingfold

Berkhampstead
Chesham
Amersham
Chalfont St. Giles
Beaconsfield
Gerrards Cross
Farnham Royal
Slough
Denham
Uxbridge
Windsor
Winkfield
Windsor Great Park
Ascot
Chobham
Bisley
Horsell
Woking
Old Woking
Mayford
Ripley
E. Clandon
E. Horsley
Shalford
Bramley
Cranleigh
Alford Crossways

Hemel Hempstead
King's Langley
Chenies
Watford
Rickmansworth
Bushey
Stanmore
Pinner
Harrow
Wembley
Northolt
Southall
Ealing
Brentford
Hounslow
Twickenham
Richmond
Kingston
Staines
Hampton
Walton
Surbiton
Esher
Hook
Ewell
Epsom
Ashtead
Leatherhead
Mickleham
Dorking
Reigate
Horley
Charlwood
Capel
Gatwick
Kingsfold
Crawley
Warnham

St. Albans
Hatfield
London Colney
S. Mimms
Radlett
Borehamwood
Elstree
Edgware
Finchley
Barnet

Chertsey
Ottershaw
Weybridge
Byfleet
Cobham
SURREY
Albury
Shere
HILLS
Leith Hill
Ewhurst
Ockley
Charlwood

0 8km
0 5miles

31	32	
19	20	
12	13	14

Broomfield
Hatfield Peverel
Tolleshunt D'Arcy
W. Mersea
Sales Pt.
Tollesbury
Blackwater
Bradwell on Sea

Chelmsford
Writtle
Maldon
B1019
B1018
B1026
B1023

A414
Gt. Baddow
Danbury
A414
Steeple
B1021

A12
Stock
A130
Cold Norton
Southminster
B1020

Res.
Rettendon
Althorne
B1012
B1010
Burnham on Crouch

Billericay
Wickford
A132
Rochford
Crouch
Foulness Pt.

twood
A129
B1013
Rayleigh
A127

Basildon
Pitsea
Hadleigh
Leigh on Sea
SOUTHEND-ON-SEA
Gt. Wakering
B1017

East Horndon
Vange
Coryton
Canvey
Shoeburyness
Shoebury Ness

Stanford le Hope
A1014
Thames
A13

Tilbury
Cliffe
B2000
I. Grain
of Grain
Sheerness
To Vlissingen

Gravesend
Hoo
Allhallows
B228
B3001

Shorne
A226
Medway
Minster
Eastchurch
Leysdown

Cobham
Strood
Gillingham
Queenborough
Sheppey
A250
Herne Bay

Rochester
Chatham
Rainham
The Swale
Whitstable

A229
Farthing Corner
M2
Sittingbourne
A2
Faversham
A299
Sturry

Snodland
Bredhurst
Key St.
Canterbury
A2

M20
Boxley
A249
Detling
Doddington
Newnham
Blean

W. Malling
Maidstone
A20
Hollingbourne
Lenham
Chilham
KENT

Wrotham Heath
A26
Harrietsham
B2077
DOWNS

Yalding
A229
A274
Charing
A252
A28

Headcorn
Pluckley
Great Chart
Elham

Paddock Wood
Marden
Staplehurst
Smarden
A28
Ashford
M20
Sellindge

Lamberhurst
Goudhurst
Sissinghurst
Biddenden
Woodchurch
Ham Street
Newingreen
Lympne

B2169
Cranbrook
Tenterden
B2067
Military Canal

To Rosslare

Cen

Strumble Hd.

Fishguard Bay

Dinas Hd.

Never

Goodwick

A487

Newp

Fishguard

Scleddau

A40

Mathry

B4313

B4313

St. David's Hd.

A487

B4330

Letterston

Wolf's Castle

15

Tufton

St. David's

Solva

Newgale

W. Cleddau

Ramsey I.

A487

B4330

B4329

St. Brides Bay

Haverfordwest

A40

Robesto Wathe

Broad Haven

B4341

B4327

Canaston Br.

Na A4

Skomer

St. Brides

7

A4076

Johnston
A 477

A4075

B

Grassholm

B4327

Milford Haven

Steynton

Cres

To Rosslare Skokholm

St. Ann's Hd.

Dale

Milford Haven

Neyland

Burton

Pembroke Dock

Angle

B4320

Pembroke

B4

St. Petrox

B4379

B4584

Lamphey

A413

Manc

Linney Hd.

St. Govans Hd.

Gwdugrug
Llansawel
Landovery
A40
B4299
B4310
B4333
Talley
Llanwrda
Cwm Wysg Res.
21
12
Cynwyl Elfed
A4063
Llangadog
B4301
Twyn-llanan
B4302
Carmarthen
A484
A485
Llanegwad
A40
Llandeilo
Black Mountain
B4300
15
B4297
B4300
1618
B4298
A40
Llanarthney
A483
Pen-y-Cae
Clears
A48
Llanddarog
Porth-y-Rhyd
A416
Llandybie
A4069
Aber
Llandyfaelog
B4306
Bryn-amman
A4069
A465
Ferryside
Tumble
Cross Hands
B4297
Ammanford
A474
Ystalyfera
Ystradgynla
Llansteph
Torwy
A484
B4309
27
A483
Pont Abraham
Glyn Ne
Kidwelly
B4317
Pontyates
A48
Llanon
Abraham
Pontardawe
Crynant
26
Bay
Pembrey
B4308
B4309
A476
Hendy
Tawe
A109
A465
Burry Port
B4431
A484
Pontardulais
A48
Resolv
A406.
Llanelli
B4296
47
M4
45
4
Glyncorrw
Llwchwr
Skewen
44
Neath
A4287
A4107
Llanmadoc
B4296
Morriston
A4271
Briton Ferry
42
B4282
4
Maesteg
Llangennith
GOWER
SWANSEA
A483
Aberavon
40
M4
Llanddewi
Gower
Upr.Killay
A4118
A4067
Black Pill
Port Talbot
Margam
Worms Hd.
A4118
Oxwich
B4436
Bishopston
Mumbles
38
A48
Pyle
Rhosili
B4247
Oxwich Bay
B4593
Swansea Bay
37
B
Port Eynon
To Cork
Porthcawl
Ogn
B4
Southern

B R I S T O L

C

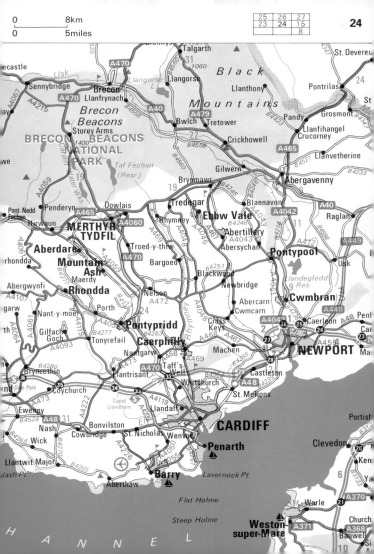

Aberystwyth

Goginan
Ponterwyd
A44
Rheidol
Pentrebont
Devils Br.
B4340
A4120
B4574
B4343
A485
B4574
Llanilar
B4575
Ystwyth
Ysbyty Ystwyth
Lledrod
Llanrhystyd
Bronnant
Ystrad
Meurig
A4340
Llansanffraid
B4337
Pontrhydfendigaid
A4343
Claer
A487
Cross
Aberaeron
Aberarth
Inn
A485
B4576
B4577
B4342
b
New Quay
38
A482
Tregaron
A487
B4342
r
Ystrad Aeron
B4342
A486
Synod Inn
Temple Bar
Llangybi
m
Teifi
Llyn
Brianne
Resr
B4338
Cribyn
A485
A4343
a
Sarnau
B4333
B4459
Llanwrtyd V
Ffostrasol
A486
Llanwnen
A475
Lampeter
779
Rhyd-Owen
B4337
A482
C
B4571
Horeb
A475
B4335
Llanybyther
Pumpsaint
Cilycwm
Llandyssul
B4336
A483
M
A484
B4459
A486
B4327
Gwyddgrug
Llansawel
Llandovery
A40
B4299
B4310
Llanwrda
B4301
Talley
A4069
Cwm
Wysg
Res.
21
Cynwyl Elfed
B4302
12
Llangadog
A484
A485
Llanegwad
A40
Twyn-llanan
Carmarthen
B4300
Llandeilo
15
Llanarthney
B4297
B4300
A483
Black
Mountain
40
A48
B4459
1618
lears
Llanddarog
B4310
A476
Llandybie
Pen-y-Cae
4298
Porth-y-Rhydd
B4306
Bryn-amman
A4069
Ferryside
Llandyfaelog
Cross
B4297
A474
A068
Aberc
B4309
Tumble
Hands
Ammanford
Ystradgynlai
Kidwelly
Pontyates
27
A483
Ystalyfera
Glyn Nea
B4304
A48
Pont
Abraham
Llan
Crynant
26
lanstephan
B4312
B4317
Sawe
A474
A4102

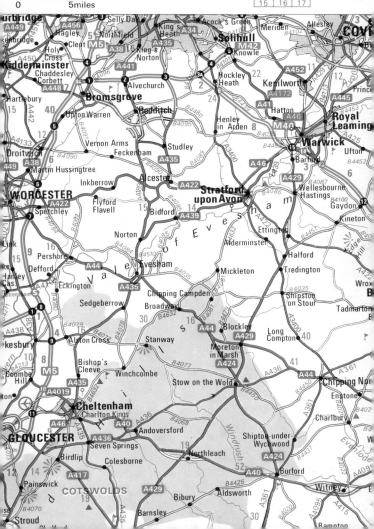

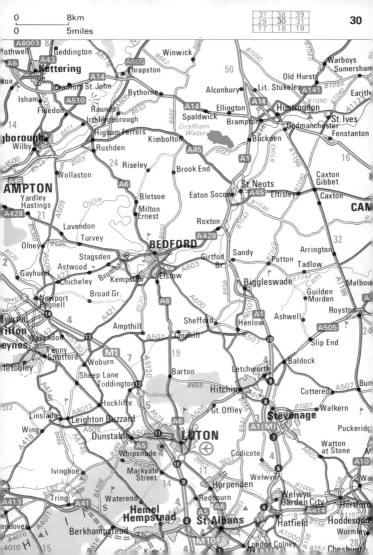

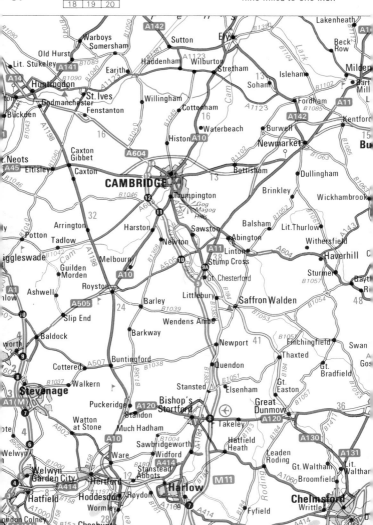

43	44	45
24	**33**	34
24	25	26

Bedagefert

487

Dolbenmaen

A498

A4085

Blaenau
Ffestiniog

A470

B4407

s

B4501

32

Tremadog

B4411

A497

Penrhyndeudraeth
Toll
Porthmadog

B4410

A496

Maentwrog

Ffestiniog

A470

B4391

B4401

Dru

Criccieth

Llyn
Trawsfynydd

Trawsfynydd

A4212

B4931

Llyn Celyn

n

s

Bala

A494

B4403

Bala L

A470

Harlech

A496

B4573

Llanbedr

32

A470

Llanuwchllyn

18
770

a

Llanaber

A496

Tyn-y-groes

L.Vyrnwy

B4403

Barmouth

Llanelltyd

A496

A493

A470

1178

Dolgellau

Cross Foxes

A470

Dinas Mawddwy

957

Banwy

37
Lla

Arthog

Cader
Idris
2927

938

Mallwyd

Llwyngwril

Aberllefenni

A470

n

t

u

Llangelynin

B4405

Corris

16

Dyfi

B4404

Llanbrynmair

A487

Tywyn

Bryn-crug

Cennaes Rd.

A489

Penegoes

Pennal

Machynlleth

Talerddig

23

Aberdyfi

A493

Carno

N

18

B4353

M
o

Pontdolgoch

Caersw

B4569

Borth

Talybont

Plynlimon
Fawr

Clywedog
Res.

B4518

Llandinam

B4572

Nant-y-moch
Res.

1350

Severn

Llandloes

13

A487

Bow Street

A4159

Aberystwyth

Goginan

A44

Rheidol

Ponterwyd

22

A470

Llangurig

9
952

B4518

Pentrebont

B4340

Devils Br.

Wye

A4120

B4574

Llanilar

A485

B4343

B4574

B4575

Ystwyth

Lledrod

Ysbyty Ystwyth

Rhavade

Llanrhystyd

d o g

y

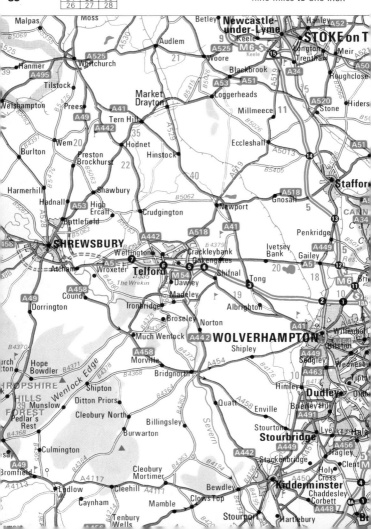

6

Benington

ston

A52

THE

WASH

Brancaster

NORFO...C...S

Hunstanton

A149

Burnham Ma...

B1153

Heacham

Docking

B155

Snettisham

B1454

Dersingham

B7155

B1335

Holbeach
Marsh

43

Gedney Drove
End

Wolferton

A479

B1153

E. Rudham

A1065

A17

B1359

Flitcham

B1440

Harpley

Ra...

4

Holbeach

Castle
Rising

Great
Massingham

Long
Sutton

Sth. Wootton

A148

Gaywood

Litcham

Sutton Br.

King's Lynn

A1101

Gayton

B1165

...ydd St. Mary

A17

Terrington
St. Clement

A149

A1078

Middleton

16

Sutton
St. James

St. John's
Highway

A47

Setchey

E. Winch

B1153

Newton

B1165

Narborough

Wend...

...ney Hill

Nene

13

A10

Nar

Necton

A47

B1169

Sth. Runcton

Wisbech

Ouse

1

Swaffham

B1077

Guyhirn

B1411

13

A134

A1122

A1065

21

Outwell

Stradsett

Hilborough

A141

A1122

Downham
Market

B1098

Nordelph

B1094

Stoke Ferry

B1160

Wissey

March

A1101

Hilgay

Methwold

A134

T   h   e

Southery

B1386

Mundford

B1099

B1093

18

Feltwell

B1386

32

Doddington

New Bedford

Old Bedford

A10

Little Ouse

Weeting

Croxto...

35

Littleport

A1101

Brandon

B1077

Chatteris

B1411

Lakenheath

Thetford

F   e   n   s

A142

Sutton

Cam

A1065

Elveden

Barnham

...sham

Ely

B1382

Beck
Row

A10...

Haddenham

A1123

Wilburton

B104

Mildenhall

20

...rith...

Stretham

13

Isleham

B1112

Icklingham

A134

Willingham

Soham

B1102

Barton
Mills

Lackford

...ngham

Cottenham

A1123

Fordham

A11

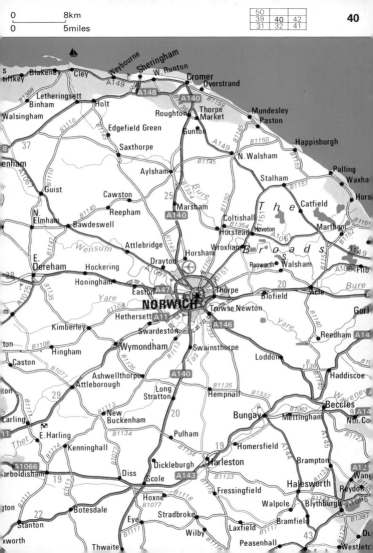

Bures • Nayland • Boxford • Kersey • Monks Eleigh • Lavenham • Hadleigh • Hintlesham • Stratford St Mary • Bramford • Capdock • Blakenham • Claydon • IPSWICH • Brightwell • Shotley • Trimley • Felixstowe • Bawdsey • Alderton • Orford • Orford Ness • Woodbridge • Melton • Ufford • Wickham Market • Farnham • Saxmundham • Tunstall • Aldeburgh • Thorpeness • Leiston • Westleton • Dunwich • Minsmere Cliffs • Walberswick • Southwold • Reydon • Wangford • Nth. Cove • Kessingland • Wrentham • Halesworth • Brampton • Blythburgh • Walpole • Bramfield • Laxfield • Peasenhall • Framlingham • Dennington • Fressingfield • Homersfield • Harleston • Pulham • Scole • Diss • Dickleburgh • Hoxne • Stradbroke • Wilby • Eye • Debenham • Thwaite • Botesdale • Redgrave • Garboldisham • E. Harling • Kenninghall • Euston • Honington • Ixworth • Stanton • Norton • Beyton • Woolpit • Gt. Finborough • Needham Market • Stowmarket • Hitcham

Sandlings

Deben • Aide • Alde • Ore

To Esbjerg & Goteborg • To Hamburg

0   8km
0   5miles

Tottington
Watton
Caston
Hingham
Attleborough
Ashwellthorpe
Wymondham
Long Stratton
Hempnall
Haddiscoe
Corton
Lowestoft

Shipdham
E. Dereham
Kimberley
Honingham
Hethersett
Swardeston
Swainsthorpe
Loddon
Reedham
Gorleston

Brisley
N. Elmham
Bawdeswell
Hockering
Easton
NORWICH
Drayton
Horsham
Lt. Se Newton
Blofield
Lingwood
Barrow Walsham
Freethorpe
Caister-on-Sea

Raynham
Fakenham
Walsingham
Guist
Cawston
Reepham
Attlebridge
Marsham
Wroxham
Coltishall
Hoveton
Horstead
N. Walsham
Stalham
Catfield
Martham
Hemsby
Ormesby St. Margaret
GREAT YARMOUTH

St. Wells
Blakeney
Binham
Letheringsett
Holt
Edgefield Green
Saxthorpe
Aylsham
Roughton
Thorpe Market
Mundesley
Paston
Happisburgh
Palling
Horsey
Waxham
Winterton

Stiffkey
Cley
Weybourne
Sheringham
W. Runton
Cromer
Overstrand

Kettle Market
To Scheveningen

B1145 B1146 A148 A1067 B1110 B1147 B1135 A1075 A1065 B1388
B1105 B1110 A149 B1149 A148 A140 B1354 B1145 B1150 B1151
A1151 A1062 A1064 A1152 A149 B1159 B1149 A1065 B1140 B1136
A11 A47 A146 A143 A12 A140 B1332 B1113 B1108 B1077 B1017
B1135 B1334 B1139 B1385 B1074

Yare
Wensum
Bure
Tas
The Broads

Carmel Hd.

Cemaes Bay

Amlwch

Point

A5025

B5111

Llanfeathlu

Alaw Res

Llanerchymedd

Llanallgo

B5110

To Dublin & Dun Laoghaire

Holyhead Bay

A5025

A n g l e s e y

B5109

Holyhead

A5

Valley B5109

Bryngwran

Cefni Res

B5109

Holy I.

B4545

Gwalchmai

Llangefni

A5114

Rhosneigr

A4080

A5025

Llanfaelog

21

B4422

A5

Llanfair

Gaerwen

A4080

Aberffraw

Bethel

B4421

B4415

Manai

B4419

Newborough

A4080

Caernarfon

Caernarfon Bay

A499

A40

Pen-y-g

Llanllyfn

Clynnog-fawr

20

A487

Llanaelhaearn

Dol

B4411

Nefyn

B4417

B4354

A499

B4417

Lleyn Peninsula

B4415

Llangwnnadl

A499

Pwllheli

Sarn Mellteyn

B4413

Cricc

Llanbedrog

Aberdaron

B4413

Abersoch

T r e m a d o c

Porth Neigwl

St.Tudwals Is.

Bay

Bardsey I.

Pencilan Hd.

0   8km
0   5miles

re

Point of

ed Wharf Bay

Puffin I.

Gt. Ormes Hd.

Llandudno

Rhos-on-Sea

Rhyl

Pres

Llangoed

Llandrillo

Colwyn Bay

B5119

A548

A547

traeth

A546

Tunnel

A55

Rhuddlan

B5429

B5109

Penmaenmawr

Conwy

Abergele

A547

A5387

St.Asaph

32

Beaumaris

A470

B5113

B5383

Llanfairfechan

15

B5113

B5382

Llanfair Talhaiarn

A541

Trefnant

Bangor

Aber

A55

A544

Llangernyw

B5382

Denbigh

Bethesda

A5

Tal-y-Cafn

19

A548

Llansannan

A543

Pentre

A366

Llyn Eigiau

Bylchau

B5384

A525

Carnedd Llywelyn

21

3484

Trefriw

Llanrwst

A542

B5435

Ll

Llyn Padarn

Llyn Ogwen

Llyn Cowlyd

A5016

1523

Alwen Res.

A543

lanberis

Capel Curig

Pass of Llanberis

A4086

993

Betws-y-Coed

B5113

1169

Pen-y-gwryd

A498

B5105

Br

Snowdon 3560

SNOWDONIA FOREST

Pentre-Foelas

A501

22

AND Dolwyddelan

NATIONAL PARK

21 1263

B4406

Cerrigydrudion

A5

32

dgelert

A470

Druid

Corw

B5401

Blaenau Ffestiniog

B4407

s

aen

A4085

A498

B4410

A496

Ffestiniog

B4401

B4397

B4402

Llandrillo

og

Maentwrog

B4391

Llanarmon Dyffr

Toll

A4212

Llyn Celyn

Porthmadog

Llyn Trawsfynydd

Bala

A494

aeudraeth

B5394

Trawsfynydd

Bala L

Llangynog

Harlech

A470

32

Llanuwchllyn

B4403

a

B4396

Llanbedr

18

770

L.Vyrnwy

Tyn-y-groes

B4393

B4393

Llanwddyn

Llanaber

Llanelltyd

A496

A470

1178

Dolmellau

54	55	56
48	49	50
37	38	39

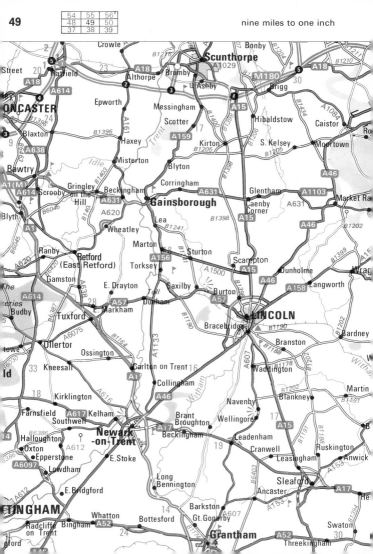

Crowle

B1216

Bonby B1204

Scunthorpe

A1029

Street 20 5 Hatfield A18 2 Althorpe 3 Brumby Ashby M180 Brigg 5 A18 B1210

A18 4 A614 Epworth Messingham A15 4 B1434 A1084

ONCASTER B1396 24 Scotter Hibaldstow Caistor Ro

3 Blaxton Haxey A159 Kirton S. Kelsey Moortown

A638 Misterton B1205 A46

Bawtry Idle Blyton B1205

A1(M) A614 Scrooby Gringley Beckingham Corringham Glentham A1103 Market Ra

Blyth on the A631 A631 Caenby A46

A1 Hill A620 **Gainsborough** Corner A15 B1202

B6045 Lea B1398 A46

Wheatley B1241

Ranby Marton Sturton Scampton A1399

Retford A156 A15 Dunholme Wrac

(East Retford) Torksey A1500 A46 A158 Langworth

Gamston E. Drayton Saxilby Burton A57

The A614 E. Markham Toll Dunham B1190 **LINCOLN** B1202

eries Budby B6387 A57 Bracebridge B1190 Bardney

Tuxford A6075 B1164 B1188 Branston With

Ollerton B1133 A607 B1178

Id 33 Kneesall Ossington Carlton on Trent 16 Waddington

18 Collingham Witham B1202 Martin

Kirklington A616 A46 Navenby Blankney B1191

Farnsfield A617 Kelham Brant Wellingore A15

Southwell A17 Broughton Leadenham 17

Halloughton **Newark** Beckingham 19 Cranwell Ruskington

Oxton A612 **-on-Trent** Leasingham Anwick

Epperstone E.Stoke A153 A17

A6097 Lowdham Long **Sleaford** He

E.Bridgford Bennington Ancaster

A612 Barkston A607 Swaton

TINGHAM Whatton A52 Bottesford Gt.Gonerby A153 Threekingham

Radcliffe Bingham **Grantham** A52

on Trent A52

dford Swaton

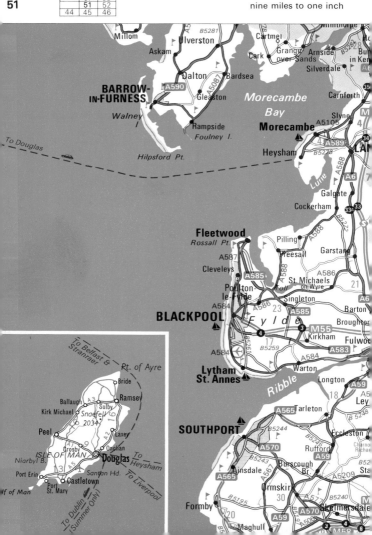

Millom
Ulverston
Askam
Cartmel
Grange over Sands
Arnside
Silverdale
Cark
B5281
Whinthorpe
B5
Bu in Ke
A6

BARROW-IN-FURNESS
Dalton
Bardsea
Gleaston
A590
A5087
Carnforth
35
M
4

Walney I.
Rampside
Foulney I.

Morecambe Bay

Morecambe
Slyne
A5105
A589
A6

To Douglas

Hilpsford Pt.

Heysham
B5278
LA

Lune
Galgate
Cockerham
A588
A6
7
33A

Fleetwood
Rossall Pt.
Pilling
Garstang
A586
A588
B6222
21
A6

Cleveleys
A587
Preesall
St Michaels on Wyre

Poulton-le-Fylde
A585
A586
Singleton
A586
A585
Barton
Broughtor

BLACKPOOL
Fylde
23
M55
3
A6
Kirkham
Fulwoo
Warton
A584
B5259
4
17
A584
A583
A584

Lytham St. Annes
Longton
A59

Ribble
18
Le

SOUTHPORT
Tarleton
A565
B5244
Eccleston
A59
Charno Richa
B52
A570
Rufford
B524
B5243
Burscough Br.
A565
A59
A5209
Ainsdale
Ormskir
B5195
Formby
A570
A577
A570
mersdal
3
M
A5
Maghull
20
30
B5240

To Belfast & Stranraer
To Douglas
To Heysham
To Liverpool
To Dublin (Summer Only)

ISLE OF MAN

Pt. of Ayre
Bride
Ramsey
Ballaugh
A3
Sulby
Kirk Michael
Snaefell
2034
Laxey
Peel
Crosby
Onchan
Douglas
Niarbyl B.
Port Erin
Santan Hd.
Castletown
Port St. Mary
f of Man

YORKSHIRE DALES

Wharfe 1392

Masham

Halton Gill Buckden

NATIONAL PARK

B6255

Ingleton

Horton in
Ribblesdale

Resr.

Kirkby Malzeard

igh
am

B6479

Arncliffe

Kettlewell

Clapham

Ramsgill

B6480

Stainforth

Malham

Grassington

Pateley
Bridge

Settle

Threshfield

Burnsall

B6265

32

Kirkby
Malham

Rylstone

B6160

Sum
Brid

B6

OF

Long
Preston

Wharfedale

Blubberhouses

A59

H

Stocks
Resr.

A65

Gargrave

ND
idburn
vton

B6478

A682

A59

Skipton

Bolton Abbey

28

Ribble

Gisburn

B6251

Earby

A629

A65

Ilkley

Burley

Otley

Waddington

34

Barnoldswick

A682

Crosshills

Silsden

19

Guisele

Clitheroe

Cowling

A6068

Keighley

A650

Barrowford

Colne

Oakworth

Bingley

Yeadon

A658

Whalley

A56

Nelson

Brierfield

Trawden

Haworth

Shipley

BRADFORD

A647

A671

A66

Gt.
Harwood

B6

A679

Padiham

BURNLEY

1425

B6141

Puds
Dri

Rishton

Clayton-le-Moors

A6114

A629

Queensbury

Wibsey

A6036

A65

Accrington

A56

A671

1334

764

21

Hebden
Bridge

A646

HALIFAX

A641

BLACKBURN

Oswaldtwistle

A56

Sowerby
Br.

A6025

Liversedge

A6

Darwen

B6232

Haslingden

Newchurch

Bacup

Todmorden

Brighouse

Beckmond

A666

B6214

Rawtenstall

A671

Ripponden

B6113

Elland

A641

Mirfi

Edgworth

Whitworth

17

A672

23

A640

Flockton

A629

Kirkbur

Tottington

Ramsbottom

A56

Littleborough

42

M62

22

HUDDERSFIELD

A642

B6213

ROCHDALE

Milnrow

A640

A62

B611

BURY

Heywood

A58

Newhey

Marsden

Meltham

Radcliffe

Whitefield

A627(M)

Royton

A672

18

Holmfirth

M62

Pendlebury

OLDHAM

Saddleworth

Denby
Dale

rton

MIDDLETON

Mossley

A635

A6024

Ingbirchwor

35

1615

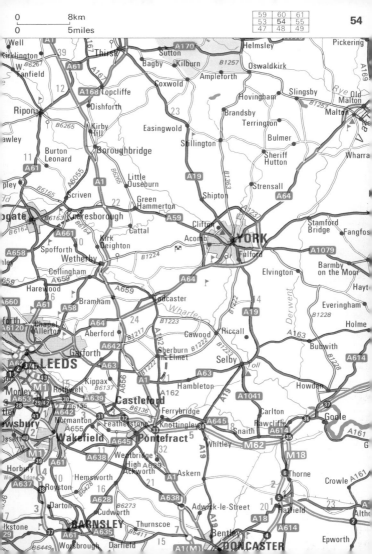

SOLWAY

Cairn Bay

nnan

Wigton

33

B5300

B5301

Red Dial

Allonby Bay

Allonby

B5299

Caldbeck

A596

Aspatria

Bothel

Ireby

Uldale

Maryport

Crosby

Flimby

A594

A595

Workington

Derwent

Cockermouth

37

A66

A596

A595

A592

Bassenthwaite Lake

13

Skiddaw .3054

754

A66

Keswick

Moresby

Distington

A5086

B5289

Derwent Water

A591

Whitehaven

Crummock Water

Buttermere

B5289

Grange

Thirlmere

Wath Brow

A595

Cleator

Ennerdale Water

Buttermere

Seatoller

A591

St. Bees Hd.

St. Bees

Egremont

LAKE DISTRICT

Scafell Pike .3206

Grasmere

Calder Br.

Wast Water

B5343

Ambl Wa

Gosforth

A595

Seascale

B5344

Eskdale Green

Duddon

Hawkshead

Drigg

66

Coniston

Conist Water

Ravenglass

Esk

Torver

A593

A5084

Ulpha

Bootle

Broughton

A595

Grizebeck

A590

Whitbeck

A5093

Greenodd

Silecroft

B5281

Millom

Ulverston

Askam

A5087

Dalton

Bardsea

BARROW-IN-FURNESS

A590

Gleaston

Mo

Lanchester
Witton
Gilbert
Houghton-le-Spring
Hetton-le-Hole
A68
Satley
B6296
Brancepeth
Brandon
DURHAM
A167
A690
6
A690
Easington
B1432
w Law
Wolsingham
Willington
A690
Crook
A689
ton-le-Wear
Wear
Weardale
Spennymoor
Ferryhill
B6291
Coxhoe
A177
A181
Trimden
Hart
A1086
Peterlee
HARTLEPOOL
A19
Bishop Auckland
A167
A688
B6282
Shildon
Sedgefield
A178
Greatham
Redca
West Auckland
A688
Newton Aycliffe
A6072
A1(M)
Wolviston
A177
MIDDLESBROUGH
A1
amdrop
A688
B6279
A68
A167
STOCKTON-ON-TEES
Toll
South Bank
Eston
B1269
Ske
Winston
B6274
Gainford
B6275
Sadberge
11
Thornaby-on-Tees
N Ormesby
A19
A171
Piercebridge
7
Long Newton
A174
Nunthorpe
Guisbo
A173
Caldwell
Stapleton
DARLINGTON
A66
A67
Yarm
A1040
Gt. Ayton
A66
Aldbrough
A66(M)
Hurworth
A167
Crathorne
B1264
Stokesley
Melsonby
Croft
Barton
Great Smeaton
A19
Hutton Rudby
Broughton
Gilling
Scotch Corner
B1263
A172
28
Richmond
A6108
Catterick Bridge
Wiske
Cleveland
NO
2
Downholme
A6136
Catterick
A684
A6108
Northallerton
B1257
Hut
Leyburn
Patrick Brompton
A684
Ainderby Steeple
A19
Wensley
Middleham
A684
Bedale
Leeming
S. Otterington
Rievaulx
ledale
A6108
B6268
Burneston
S. Kilvington
Helm
Masham
Kirklington
Well
A1
39
Thirsk
A170
Sutton
Kilburn
B1257
Osv
Ure
W. Tanfield
A61
A167
Bagby
Ampleforth
Kirkby Malzeard
A168
Topcliffe
12
Coxwold
Hovin
gill
Ripon
Dishforth
23
Brandsby

0	8km
0	5miles

altburn
Brotton
Loftus Staithes
ingdale
Hinderwell *Runswick Bay*
B1366 B1266 A174
31 A171 Lythe A174 Whitby
Danby
Castleton Egton Sleights High Hawsker
B1416 Robin Hood's Bay
Goathland 1930
YORK MOORS Ravenscar
ONAL PARK 20
A171
Rosedale *Derwen*
Abbey
ole Lastingham A169 Cloughton Burniston
moorside Middleton Scalby **Scarborough**
Simmington A170 A165
A170 Pickering 44 Allerston Seamer Cayton
Thornton Brompton Wykeham B1261 A1039
Dale B1415 A64 Folkton 18 Filey
Yedingham Staxton A1039 Muston
B1258 Ganton Hunmanby
Slingsby Old A64 Sherburn Reighton
Rye Malton W. Heslerton Foxholes North Burton Bempton
B1258 Rillington *of Pickering* *Wolds* A165
Maltor 41 uston

Ailsa Craig

New Dailly
Old Dailly
B741
Girvan

B734

C a r r i

51
A77
Barr
1281
Polmaddie
Hill
Lendalfoot
A714

Cree

Colmonell
B734
Stinchar
Barrhill
Tig
559
B7027
A714
Ballantrae
Ba
L. Dorna
Beneraird
1435
Glen App
G a l
Bladnoch

To Larne
Corsewall Pt.
The Moors
Luce
Taff
B738
Kirkcolm
A718
B79
Loch Ryan
Cairnryan
A77
N
Sl
58
Leswalt
B738
The
New Luce
Black
Kirkc
Stranraer
Cas.Kennedy
A77
A75
Glenluce
To Douglas (Summer Only)
Rinns
A757
A747
A764
A716
Mochrum
L.
Portpatrick
B7005
of
Stoneykirk
Galloway
Sandhead
A747
Kirk of
Mochrum
Port William
L u c e
Port Logan
B716
B7065
B a y
Drummore
B7041
Mull of Galloway

72	73	74
64	65	66
	57	58

Sanquhar

Mennock

Menno

2403

Durisdeer

Moffat

Capplegill Ettrick Pen · 2268

96

Beattock

B709

1096

Carronbridge

Thornhill

Penpont

Tynron

oniaive A702

A76

Closeburn

Boreland

69

Corrie
Common

Parkgate

Templand

Dunscore

L. Urr

Lochmaben

Lockerbie

A701 A709

Locharbriggs

A74

Ecclefechan

Maxwelltown

Torthorwald

Dumfries

A75

Dalton

Crocketford

Mouswald

Kirk
Flem

Springholm

Glencaple

Bankend

Clarencefield

33

Annan

Gretna Gree

ossmichael

18

A75

Cummertrees

Dornock

Eastriggs

New Abbey

Port
Carlisle

Criffell
1866

Dalbeattie

Moricambe
Bay

Kirkbride

Palnackie

Kirkbean

Newton
Arlosh

encairn

Kippford

Oulton

ght

*Southerness
Pt.*

Silloth

Wigton

Dundrennan

Auchencairn Bay

Beckfoot

Abbey
Town

33

Red
Dial

S O L W A Y

F I R T H

*Allonby
Bay*

Allonby

Aspatria

Bothel

Ireby

Caldb

A596

Maryport

Crosby

Uldale

Flimby

Cockermouth

37

Bassenthwaite

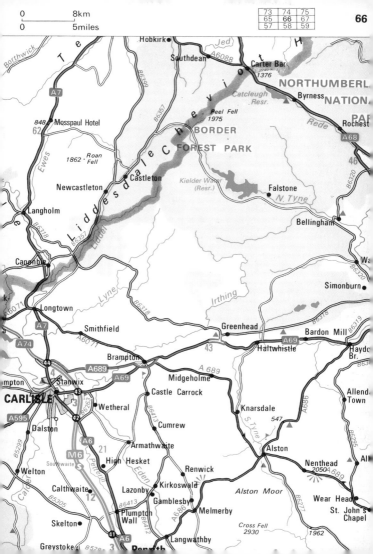

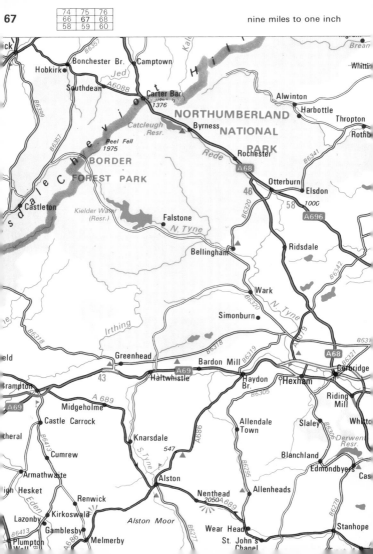

0   8km
0   5miles

Aln

Longhoughton

Alnwick

B6341

Lesbury

A1

Alnmouth

Edlingham

Alnmouth Bay

Newton on the Moor

Warkworth

Amble

B6341

B6344

B6345

B6345

Acklington

19

Longframlington

Felton

22

Coquet

B6427

A697

Longhorsley

Ugham

Druridge Bay

Netherwitton

B1337

Ellington

Longhirst

artburn

B6343

Morpeth

Ashington

Mitford

A197

Newbiggin-by-the-Sea

Wansbeck

Whalton

B6524

A196

Bedlington

Belsay

A1

Stannington

18

Blyth

Blyth

16

Cramlington

B6309

A696

Seaton Delaval

A192

Whitley Bay

Ponteland

B6323

Earsdon

A19

Tynemouth

Heddon on the Wall

A69

Killingworth

Longbenton

Walsend

17

Gosforth

S.Shields

Tyne

Ryton

NEWCASTLE

UPON TYNE

Tyne Tunnel

Jarrow

Hebburn

Newburn

Prudhoe

Blaydon

Gateshead

Boldon

A695

Whickham

Felling

Whitburn

B6315

B6309

Burnopfield

A1231

A184

A694

Washington

SUNDERLAND

otley

Ebchester

A692

Birtley

A1(M)

A182

New Seaham

Br.

A6076

A167

Stanley

A693

Chester-le-Street

A183

Ryhope

Leadgate

Consett

A693

Houghton-le-Spring

Seaham

Lanchester

Witton Gilbert

Hetton le Hole

B6296

A691

A167

A690

Easington

A68

14

DURHAM

5

Satley

Haswell

Tow Law

B6299

Brancepeth

A690

B1283

A181

Peterlee

Wolsingham

Brandon

B6291

A181

A1

To Bergen (Summer Only)

To Stavanger (Summer Only)

2571
Paps of Jura

Sou

Sanaigmore

Port Askaig

Feolin

Craighouse

Gruinart

L. Gruinart

Sound of Islay

A846

A846

Ballygrant

I s l a y

A846

Bridgend

Port Charlotte

L. Indaal

Bowmore

A847

Ardtalla

Portnahaven

A846

A8016

Gigha I

Rinns Pt.

Ardminis

Port Ellen

Ardbeg

The Oa

Mull of Oa

Bellocha

Machrihanish

Rathlin I.

Mull of Kintyre

Dunoon

GREEN

Port Gla

A770

A78

Port Gia

Tighnabruaich

Colintraive

Kames

Innellan

Inverkip

B888

Gry

Tarbert

Port Bannatyne

Wemyss Bay

W. Tarbert

Skelmorlie

B

Kennacraig

Ardlamont Pt.

thesay

Ascog

B74

Whitehouse

B8001

33

Largs

Lochwinno

52

Inchmarnock

Gt. Cumbrae I.

Skipness

Millport

A760

Kilbirnie

achan

B842

B896

Claonaig

Sd. of Bute

Lit. Cumbrae I.

Fairlie

Dalry

A737

Summer Only

Kilchattan

A78

rossaig

Lochranza

A841

B781

B780

W. Kirbride

Auche

Pirnmill

Sannox

Seamill

Kilwinning

B778

Goat Fell 2866

Corrie

dale

A841

Ardrossan

Stevenston

B880

Brodick

Saltcoats

Dro

n

Irvine Bay

Blackwaterfoot

A r r a n

Lamlash

F I R T H

Troon

B74

Holy I.

A841

O F

Prestwick

Whiting Bay

C L Y D E

Lagg

AYR

Pladda I.

A719

B7024

Culzean Castle

Maybole

A77

Maidens

A713

Turnberry

Kirkoswald

Cro

B741

New Dailly

Ailsa Craig

Old Dailly

Girvan

Kilbrannan Sound

Kyles of Bute

B u t e

A83

A815

A844

A841

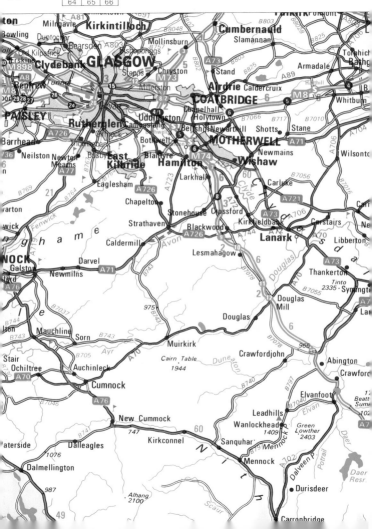

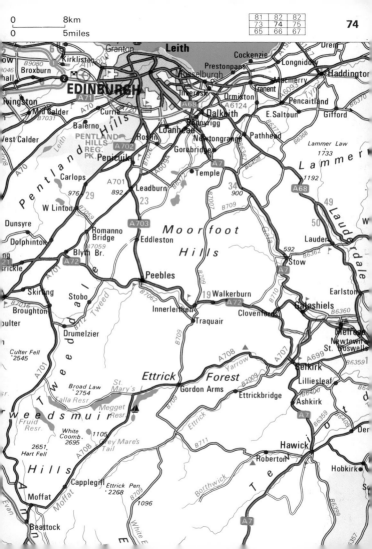

0   8km
0   5miles

Granton   **Leith**   Cockenzie   Oren
Kirkliston   Prestonpans   Longniddry
B9080   Broxburn   Musselburgh   Macmerry   Haddington
ow   1046   hall   **EDINBURGH**   Inveresk   Tranent   Pencaitland
A71   Ormiston   A6124   Gifford
ingston   A70   Mid Calder   Currie   A720   Dalkeith   E. Saltoun
B7031   Balerno   A68   Bonnyrigg   Pathhead   B6368
West Calder   PENTLAND   Roslin   Loanhead   Newtongrange
HILLS   REG.   A702   Lammer Law   1733
PK.   Penicuik   Gorebridge   A7   Lammer
Leith   1192   A68
Carlops   A701   Temple   34   49
976   29   892   Leadburn   900
W Linton   23   B709   50
Dunsyre   A703   *Moorfoot*   Lauder   W
Romanno   Eddleston   *Hills*   592   B6362
Dolphinton   Bridge   B7059   Stow   A7
rickle   21   Blyth Br.   Peebles   Earlston
A72   Skiring   Stobo   19   Walkerburn   Galashiels
B7062   A72   B710   B6360
Broughton   Innerleithen   Clovenfords
oulter   Drumelzier   Traquair   Melrose
Culter Fell   2545   *Tweed*   A708   Newtown   St. Boswells
Ettrick   *Forest*   A699   B6359
Weedsmuir   St.   Gordon Arms   Selkirk   Lilliesleaf
Broad Law   2754   Mary's L.   Ettrickbridge   Ashkirk   A7
Talla Resr.   Megget   B709   B6359
Fruid   Resr.   White   1105   B711   Hawick
2651   Coomb   2695   Grey Mare's   *Te*
Hart Fell   A708   Tail   Roberton   Hobkirk
Hills   Capplegill   Ettrick Pen   Borthwick   B6399
Moffat   2268   B709   1096   A7
Evan   White E   Beattock

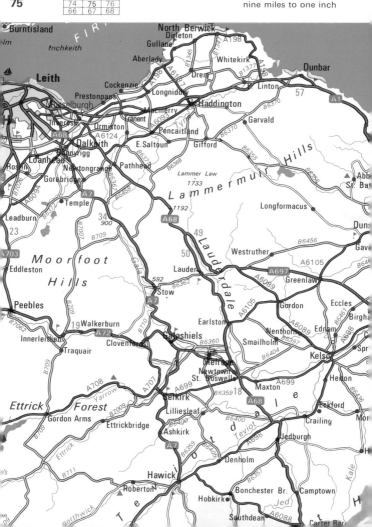

nspath
St. Abb's Hd.
A1107 *B6438*
St. Abb's
antshouse
Coldingham   Eyemouth
                    Burnmouth
B6355
2   Ayton
B6437 *B6355* *B6460*
on Chirnside
            A6105
Whiteadder
2   *B6461*   **Berwick-**
B6437   **upon-Tweed**
ton *Tweed*
            B6364   Spittal
Norham   A1167
                    A1
6112   Ancroft   Beal
am   Duddo   *Holy Island*
    Cornhill   *Budle Bay*
Wark on Tweed Etal *B6353*
                Ford   Lowick   *Farne Islands*
B6352   30
B6351   Belford *B1342* Bamburgh
Kirknewton Doddington   Seahouses
etholm   North   Beadnell
        Wooler Chatton Sunderland *B1340*
                B6349 Warenford *Beadnell Bay*
        A697   *B6348*
            Chillingham
The Cheviot
2676   46   Eglingham   *B6347*
                    B6347   Embleton
                    B6346   *B1339*
    Ingram
Breamish   *Aln*   Longhoughton
Whittingham   Lesbury
                Alnwick A1   Alnmouth
Alwinton   Edlingham *B6341*   *Alnmouth Bay*
            Newton on Warkworth

Trochry
Meikleour
Murthly
Capu
Meikleour
Strath Braan
Waterloo
Bankfoot
Amulree
Ardeonaig
Glen Almond
Stanley
Guildtown
Resr.
Balbeggie
A9
B8063
Almond
New Sc
Methven
St. Fillans
Bridgend
Earn
Comrie 53
Gilmerton
A85
PERTH
Glencars
Crieff
Cherrybank
Br.
Vorlich
3224
Glen Artney
Muthill
A9
Abern
Aberargie
Dunning
Gleneagles Hotel
Auchterarder
Blackford
33
Braco
Greenloaning
Glen Devon
Glendevon 51
Milnathort
Kinross
Kinross
allander
Falls of
Black Linn
Glen
Eagles
A823
Leven
49
Drumvaich
Doune
Yetts of Muckart
A9
42
ntexh
A84
Dunblane
Rumbling Br.
Cleish Hills
Kelty
nhill
A826
Bridge of Allan
Alva
Dollar
Devon
M90
Kippen
Menstrie
Tillicoultry
Saline
Gargunnock
Tullibody
STIRLING
Alloa
Cow
Gargunnock Hills
St. Ninians
Clackmannan
A977
A907
DUNFERMLINE
Bannockburn
Kincardine
Crossgates
Aber
try
Stirling
Airth
Culross
A985
Cairneyhill
A921
Plean
Torryburn
Rosyth
Inverkeithin
B818
Stenhousemuir
Bo'ness
Queensferry
Carron Resr.
Denny
Larbert
Grangemouth
Blackness
Toll
S. Queensfe
Kilsyth
A803
Camelon
A904
Cumbernauld
Falkirk
Polmont
Linlithgow
Kirkliston
Slamannan
B825
B9080
Broxbury
Mollinsburn
Uphall
ngnggs
A73
Torphichen
Bathgate
EDINB
OW
Stand
Armadale
Livingston
A71
Chryston
A89
Blackburn
Mid Calder
Cu
Millerston
Airdrie
Caldercruix
M8
Balerno
COATBRIDGE
Whitburn
West Calder
PENTL
HILLS

0   8km
0   5miles

Coupar
Angus

Hills

Nowrye

Todhills

14

Muirdrum

Arbroath

A92

B878

B961

Barry

Carnoustie

B954

rrelton

B923

Muirhead

B930

Monifieth

aw

B953

Longforgan

DUNDEE

Toll

Broughty Ferry

Inchture

A85

Newport-on-Tay

Tayport

Errol

rse of Gowrie

Wormit

B946

Firth of Tay

B945

ewburgh

Kilmany

Leuchars

A92

Lindores

Balmullo

St. Andrews

936

B937

Dairsie

A914

Eden

A917

Kingsbarns

Cupar

A913

B939

30

ermuchty

A91

Ceres

Pitscottie

A915

Howe of

B940

Fife

Ladybank

Crail

Kilrenny

REGIONAL

Kettlebridge

B927

Largo Ward

B940

PARK

25

Colinsburgh

B941

B9171

A917

Anstruther

Leslie

A92

Markinch

Largo

Kilconquhar

Pittenweem

Glenrothes

A911

Leven

Elie

St. Monans

I. of May

ssie

Thornton

A915

Buckhaven

A92

E. Wemyss

elly

Dysart

ath

KIRKCALDY

FIRTH OF FORTH

B9157

A921

Fidra

Bass Rock

Kinghorn

Burntisland

North Berwick

olm

Inchkeith

Dirleton

A198

Gullane

Aberlady

B1345

Whitekirk

A198

Dunbar

B1377

Drem

Leith

Cockenzie

A198

A6137

Linton

57

Prestonpans

Longniddry

A1

Musselburgh

Macmerry

B6370

3H

Tranent

Haddington

A6093

Inveresk

Ormiston

Garvald

A68

A6124

Pencaitland

B6370

Dalkeith

E. Saltoun

Gifford

B6355

Roslin

Loanhead

Nwrig

Pathhead

B6368

Hills

Newtongrange

Lammer Law

Hills

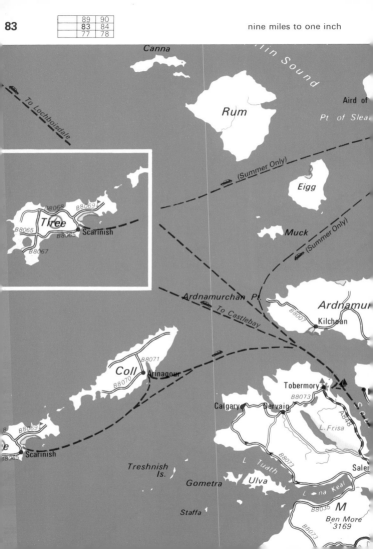

Canna

Rum

To Lochboisdale

Aird of

Pt of Slea

(Summer Only)

Eigg

B8068   B8069

Tiree
B8065
B8067   Scarinish

Muck   (Summer Only)

Ardnamurchan Pt.

Ardnamur

To Castlebay   B8007   Kilchoan

B8071

Coll   Arinagour
B8070

Tobermory

Calgary   Dervaig   B8073

B8069   L. Frisa

e
B8065   Scarinish

Treshnish
Is.   L Tuath   B8073   Saler

Gometra   *Ulva*   L na Keal

Staffa   B8035   **M**
Ben More
3169
B8073

Kinloch Hourn

L. Cluanie

L. Loyne

Glen Loyne

Glen Garry

Glen Garry

Fort Augustus

Glen Mo

Oich

A82

Glen Tarff

A87 Invergarry

L. Oich

Tomdoun Hotel

L. Garry

L. Quoich

Glen

Murlaggan

B8005

L. Arkaig

L. Lochy

Glen Roy

Roy

L. Laggan

Gairlochy

B8004

Spean Br.

Roybridge

47

A86

Glen Spean

b

BEN ALDE

an

A830

Lochy

A82

Corpach

A861 Loch Eil

Fort William

Ben Nevis 4408

GLEN NEVIS

Glen

c

h

a

L. Treig

L. Ossian

P I A N

N

Corran

Loch Linnhe

L

O

Leven

Kinlochleven

Blackwater Res

B863

M

Onich

N.Ballachulish

861

Kentallen

Ballachulish

Glencoe

Glen Coe

50

Kingshouse Hotel

L. Laidon

Moor of

L. Eigheach

A828

Appin

Bidean nam Bian 3766

Glen Etive

GLENCOE

G

R

Rannoch

1036

L. Giorr

49

tnacroish

3602

L. Tulla

L. Lyon

Barcaldine

Etive

Ben Starav 3541

Bridge of Orchy

1033

L. Giorr

Loch

Bonawe

Ben Cruachan 3689

Glen Orchy

B8074

A82

Tyndrum

A85

Glen Loc

Lochay

B

Taynuilt

Pass of

B8077

Loch Awe Strasmilchon

0   8km
0   5miles

Brackburn
B9126
Bucksburn
Echt   Elrick
ABERDEEN
B9119   Lumphanan   A944
land   B9993   Garlogie   Cults
B9004   59   Torphins   B977   B9125   Bieldside
Kincardine   A980   Peterculter   A93   B9077
O'Neil   Maryculter   B9077   A92   Portlethen
Dee   B993   Hillside
Aboyne   Cammachmore   A92
Marywell   B976   Banchory   B9077
Strachan   Muchalls
W. of Feugh
Mowtie
Kerloch   A957
1747
W. of Dye   t   h
Cairn o' Mount   Stonehaven
1488   Auchinblae   A94
un   Esk   Roadside
Fettercairn   B966   B967
N Esk   B9120   Inverbervie
st Water   Edzell   B974   The   Laurencekirk
Inchbare   B966   Mearns   St. Cyrus   53
Marykirk   A92
r   e   Brechin   A837
dice   A935
S. Esk   Montrose
B9134   A933
A934
Friockheim   Lunan B
Inverkeilor
B9928   B961   A923
B927   Marywell
Arbroath
Muirdrum   A92
Barry   B930
Carnoustie
nnifieth

103	103	98
103	89	90
	83	34

Rubha Hunish

Score B

Kilmaluag

A855

Staffin

Uig

Dunvegan Hd.

Geary

Loch Snizort

Stein

B886

The Storr 2360

Kensaleyre

A855

Milovaig

L Dunvegan

Dunvegan

A850

Edinbane

Bernisdale

Carbost

B884

Roskhill

Portree

Macleod's Tables

A850

B885

A850

Bracadale

S k y e

B883

L Bracadale

Harport

Fiskavaig

B8009

Drynoch

Scons

Carbost

A863

A850

Sligachan Hotel

Cuillin Hills 3257 Sgurr Alasdair

Blaver 3042

L Coruisk

Glenbrittle

S E A

O F   T H E

L Brittle

Soay

L Scavaig

B8083

Elgol

Tars

B R I D E S

Canna

Cuillin Sound

Vaternish Pt.

ain

0   8km

0   5miles

Poolewe

STRATHNASHEALLAG

Fionn
Loch

Gair Loch   Gairloch

Loch Maree
Hotel

A832

Slioch
3217

LOCH MAREE

Rona

Diabaig

Ben Eighe
3309

TORRIDON

Kinlochewe

A890

815

L. a'Chrois

Inveralligin

3456

Torridon

Upr
L. Torridon

Shieldaig

BEN DAMPH

L.
Damh

APPLECROSS

Beinn
Bhan
*2936

Glen Carron

Applecross

Inner Sound

2054

Lochcarron

Achintee

Raasay

Toscaig

Kishorn

L Kishorn

L Carron

Ling

L. Me

Plockton

Stromeferry

A890

Scalpay

Duirinish

Elchaig

Falls of
Glomach

Mam Soul
3862

L. Aff

Kyle of Lochalsh

A87

Dornie

KINTAIL

Kyleakin

A850

L. Alsh

Inverinate

Ben Attow
*3383

Broadford

Breakish

(Summer
Only)

Loch Duich

Affric

Isle
Oronsay

A851

Kylerhea

Glenelg

Shiel Bridge

Invershiel

Glen Shiel

L. Aff

ishort

GLENELG

A87

Cluanie
889 Br

Teangue

Arnisdale

L. Cl

Armadale
dvasar

Loch Hourn

Sd of Sleat

Airor

Kinloch
Hourn

Glen
Glen

KNOYDART

STRATHNASHEALLAG
Poolewe
Fionn Loch
Falls of Measach
1110
Beinn 3547
Gairloch
ir Loch
021
755
B8056
L. a Braoin
Sgurr Mor 3637
Loch Maree Hotel
A832
L. Fannich
Slioch 3217
LOCH MAREE
Diabaig
Ben Eighe 3309
Kinlochewe
L. a'Chroisg
Achnasheen
815
Strath B
A87
TORRIDON
3456
Inveralligin
Torridon
Upr L Torridon
Shieldaig
L. Damh
BEN DAMPH
Glen Carron
L. Monar
CROSS
Beinn Bhan 2936
A890
054
Lochcarron
Achintee
Kishorn
L Carron
Sgurr na Lapaich 3773
L Kishorn
Plockton
Ling
canni
aig
Stromeferry
A890
Duirinish
L. Mullardoch
Glen Cannich
L. Beinn a'Mheadhoin
Ish
A87
Dornie
Elchaig
Falls of Glomach
Mam Soul 3862
L. Affric
L Alsh
L. Aish
KINTAIL
Inverinate
(Summer Only)
ylerhea
Glenelg
Loch Duich
Invershiel
Ben Attow 3383
Glen Affric
Affric
Shiel Bridge
GLENELG
Glen Shiel
A87
Cluanie 889 Br
84
Torgy
A8
Glen
Fo
Arnisdale
L. Cluanie
79
Loch Hourn
Kinloch Hourn
L. Loyne
Glen Garry
A87 Inverg
KNOYDART
Glen Loyne
Glen

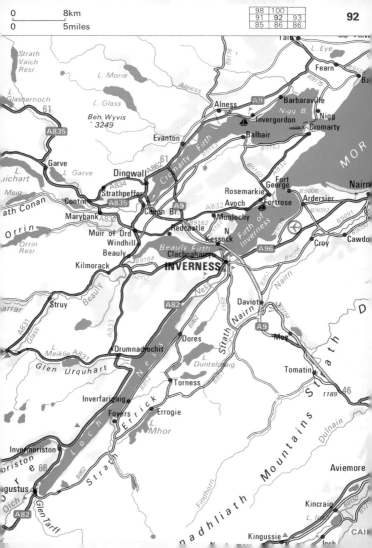

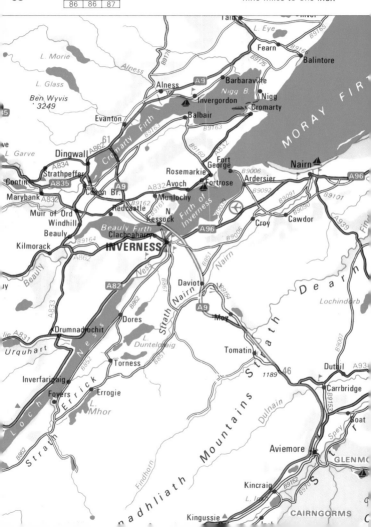

MORAY FIRTH

L. Morie

L. Glass

Ben Wyvis
· 3249

L Garve

Talk

L. Eye

Fearn

Balintore

B9175

B9166

B9176

Alness

Barbaraville

Nigg B.

Nigg

Invergordon

Cromarty

Balblair

Evanton

A9

B9163

Dingwall

Cromarty Firth

Strathpeffer

A834

Contin

A835

61

B9162

Rosemarkie

Fort George

B9006

Nairn

A96

Marybank

A832

Cong Br.

A9

Avoch

Fortrose

Ardersier

B9092

B9091

B9101

A939

Muir of Ord

Redcastle

Munlochy

N.

Firth of Inverness

B9090

Cawdor

Windhill

B9161

Kessock

A96

Croy

B9006

Beauly

Clachnaharry

INVERNESS

B9164

Kilmorack

A862

Beauly Firth

Beauly

Ness

Nairn

Dearth

A833

Ness

Strath Nairn

Daviot

B862

B851

A82

Lochinderb

Drumnadrochit

Urquhart

A831

Dores

L. Duntelchaig

Moy

A9

B9007

Tomatin

Duthil

A93

Loch Ness

Inverfarigaig

Torness

B851

1189

46

Carrbridge

Foyers

Errogie

Dulnain

B9153

L. Mhor

Strath Errick

Boat

Monadhliath Mountains

Spey

Aviemore

GLENMO

Findhorn

Kincraig

B9152

B9070

Kingussie

CAIRNGORMS

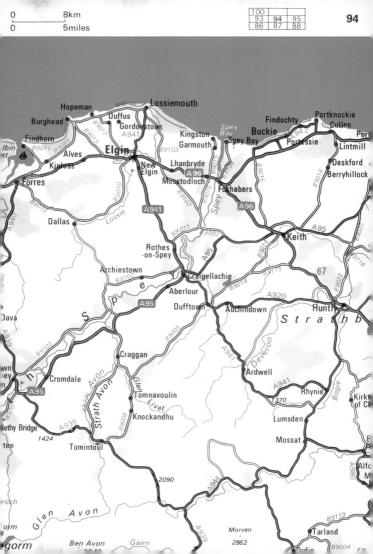

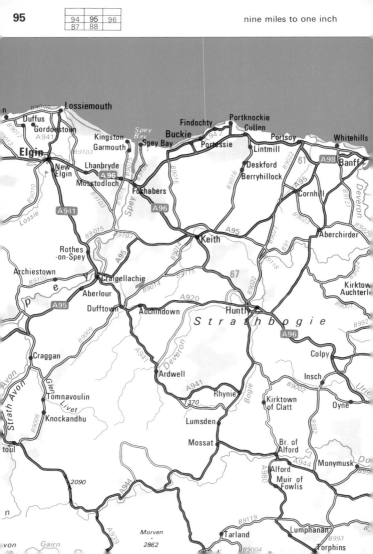

Lossiemouth

Duffus
Gordonstown
B9040
B9012
A941
n
Elgin
New
Elgin
A96
Mosstodloch
Lhanbryde
Kingston
Garmouth
Spey
Bay
Spey Bay
Fochabers
A96
A941
Lossie
B9010
B9103
B9015
B9103
Spey
Findochty
Portknockie
Buckie
Cullen
Portsoy
Portessie
A942
Whitehills
Lintmill
61
A98
Banff
Deskford
Berryhillock
B9018
B9022
A95
Cornhill
Deveron
B9121
Aberchirder
B9023
Keith
A95
Rothes
-on-Spey
Archiestown
e
A95
p
Aberlour
Dufftown
Craigellachie
B9102
B9014
B9009
Auchindown
A920
67
B9002
Hunt
S t r a t h b o g i e
A96
Kirktow
Auchterl
B9001
B992
Colpy
Craggan
Ardwell
A941
Deveron
Rhynie
Bogie
Kirktown
of Clatt
Insch
B9002
Urie
Oyne
B902
Tomnavoulin
Glen
Livet
Knockandhu
B9008
A941
370
Lumsden
Mossat
Br. of
Alford
A944
Monymusk
B99
Strath
Avon
toul
2090
A944
Alford
A980
Muir of
Fowlis
Do
n
Morven
2862
B9119
Tarland
Lumphanan
B993
Torphins
von
Gairn
A939
B9004

0   8km
0   5miles

uff
rdenstown   Pennan   Rosehearty   Fraserburgh
Longmanhill   Inverallochy
              New   A92   St. Combs
              Aberdour   Rathen
                        A98
                                                        Crimond
              New
              Pitsligo   Strichen   A952
        Newbyth   B9093   18
        Cuminestown
                    B u c h a n   Mintlaw   Ugie   Peterhead
riff   New Deer   Old   A950
                              Deer   Burnhaven
                                        Clola
                                                43
        Fyvie
        Methlick   A92   Cruden Bay
                                    Yth   33   Cruden Bay
        arves   Ellon
                    B995   A920
        Oldmeldrum   Colliestoun
                        B9000
                                    Newburgh
erurie
              Newmachar   To Lerwick & Stromness
              B977
                        A92
mnay   Kintore
        A96   Dyce
        Blackburn
              Bucksburn
        Elrick   ABERDEEN
        Garlogie   A944
        Cults
        Rualdside

0   8km
0   5miles

Pt. of Stoer

Clashnessie
Culkein
Drumbeg
B869
Oldany
Eddrachillis Bay
Kylesku
A894
Quinag
L. Glencoul
A894
Kylestrome
Badcall
Scourie
Handa
A894
Laxford Br.
Ben Stack 2364
Arkle 2580
Foinaven
Rhiconich
Reay Forest
L. Stack
L. More
A838
Dionard
A838
Kinlochbervie
B801
Cape Wrath
The Parbh
Kyle of Durness
A838
Durness
Smoo
63
L. Eriboll
Eriboll

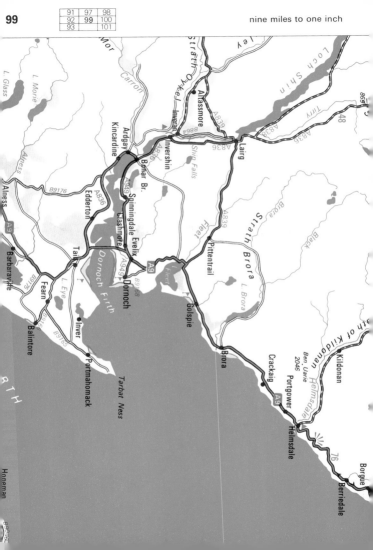

Scrabster
Thurso
Forss
A836
B870
Halkirk
Myphster
Castletown
A882
Roadside
A836
B874
A895
Watten
L. Watten
Dunnet Head
Scarfskerry
Dunnet
L. Heilen
A836
Lochside
Killimster
Reiss
Billster
Keiss
Freswick
Bruan
A9
Wick
Sinclairs B
Gills
John o' Groats
Duncansby Hd.
Hun
Stroma

Latheron
Achavanich
Lybster
Occumster
Janetstown
Dunbeath
Bourgue
Berriedale
Dunbeath
2313
Thurso
Calde

To Aberdeen
To Lerwick

ORKNEY

Dunnet Head
To Scrabster
Brough Hd.
The Barony
Marwick Hd.
Skara Brae
Birsay
Rousay
Westray
Papa Westray
Nth. Ronaldsay Firth
North Ronaldsay
Hoy
Ward Hill 1570
Lyness
Greamsay
Stromness
Stenness
L. of Stenness
A967
Dounby
L. of Harray
A986
Scapa
Flow
Scapa
A965
Kirkwall
Shapinsay
Eday
Backaland
Egilsay
Stronsay
Whitehall
Sanday
Auskerry
Burray
St. Margaret's Hope
South Ronaldsay
Burwick Brough Ness
Copinsay
Deerness
Tankerness
Mainland
Pentland Firth
Waterinho
Firth
St. Mary's
B9061
Stroma
North Sd.
The
Nth. Ronaldsay Firth
Mull Head
Firth
Shaill

0 _____ 8km
0 _____ 5miles

To Torshavn (Summer Only)

To Lerwick

Rora Hd.

Tor Ness

Rackwick

Ward Hill 1565 ▲

H o y

Lyness

B9047

Wall

Cantick Hd.

Swona

Graemsay

Hoy Sound

Stromness

A965

Yesnaby

Marwick Hd.

B9056

Twatt

Birsay

A966

Brough Hd.

A967

A986

L. of Stenness

A967

Dounby

Swann.

B9057

Finstown

Woodwick

A966

Evie

Eynhallow Sound

Washster

Rousay

B9064

Ward Hill

Orphir

A965

B. of Firth

Widl Firth

Tingwall

Birsay

Wyre

Gairsay

Eglisay

Eday

Linga Holm

Flotta

Cava

Fara

Sd. of Hoxa

Scapa Flow

A964

Kirkwall

Mary's

A961

St.

A960

A961

Shapinsay

Balfour

Veantro

B9058

Shapinsay Sound

Stronsay Firth

Eday Sd.

Soul Ness

Braeswick

B9063

Bay of Holland

Whitehall

B9060

Stronsay

Papa Stronsay

Sanday Sound

Pentland Firth

Burwick

Old Head

Brough Ness

Grim Ness

St. Margaret's Hope

S. Ronaldsay

Burray

A9061

A961

Rose Ness

B9052

B9050

B9051

Deer Sd.

Skaill

Pt. of Ayre

Mull Hd.

Rerwick Hd.

Auskerry Sd.

Lamb Hd.

Copinsay

Auskerry

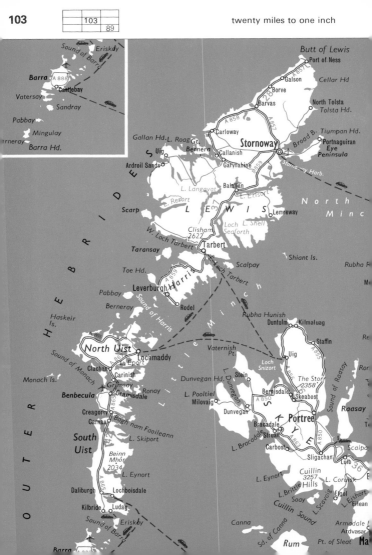

Butt of Lewis
Port of Ness
Cellar Hd.
Galson
Borve
Barvas
North Tolsta
Tolsta Hd.
Carloway
Stornoway
Sound of Barra
Eriskay
Barra
Castlebay
Vatersay
Sandray
Pabbay
Mingulay
Barra Hd.
Berneray
Gallan Hd.
L. Roag
Gt.
Bernera
Callanish
Garynahine
Uig
Ardroil Sands
L. Langavat
LEWIS
Balallan
L. Erisort
Lemreway
Broad B.
Tiumpan Hd.
Portnaguiran
Eye
Peninsula
Stornoway Harb.
North
Minc
Scarp
L. Resort
W. Loch Tarbert
Clisham
2622
Loch
Seaforth
L. Shell
Taransay
Tarbert
Scalpay
Shiant Is.
Rubha R
Toe Hd.
Harris
Loch Tarbert
Me
Leverburgh
Pabbay
Berneray
Sound of Harris
Rodel
Rubha Hunish
Duntulm
Kilmaluag
Haskeir
Is.
Vaternish
Pt.
Staffin
Uig
The Storr
2358
Ror
North Uist
Lochmaddy
Clachan
Eport
Carinish
Grimsay
Ronay
Sound of Monach
Monach Is.
Benbecula
Craigmsale
Dunvegan Hd.
Stein
Milovaig
L. Pooltiel
Loch
Snizort
Bernisdale
Skeabost
Dunvegan
L. Dunvegan
Raasay
Sound of Raasay
Portree
Creagorry
Carnaa
Bagh nam Faoileann
Braca dale
Struan
Carbost
SKYE
A 850
Te
South
Uist
L. Skiport
Beinn
Mhòr
2034
L. Eynort
L. Brocadale
Sligachan
Luib
36
Cuillin
3257
Hills
L. Coruisk
Scalpa
Daliburgh
Lochboisdale
L. Eynort
Cuillin Sound
L. Brittle
L. Scavaig
Soay
Egol
L. Erishort
Erlean
Kilbride
Ludag
Eriskay
Sound of Barra
Canna
Sd. of Canna
Rum
Pt. of Sleat
Armadale
Ardvasar
Ma
Barra
OUTER
HEBRIDES
Little
Minch

0   30km
0   20miles

Muckle Flugga
Burra Firth
Herma Ness
Norwick
Haroldswick
Baltasound
Balta
Unst
A 968
Cullivoe
Uyeasound
Dalsetter
Belmont
Uyea
Gutcher
To Seydhisfjordhur & Torshavn (Summer Only)
Mid Yell
Fetlar
Isbister
Yell Sound
South-haa
W.
Yell
Funzie
Sandwick
Colla Firth
Fetlar Sd.
The Faither
Otterswick
North Collafirth
Ollaberry
Burravoe
Esha Ness
Hillswick
Heoga Ness
Stenness
A 970
Mossbank
Out Skerries
Scatsta
St Magnus Bay
A 968
Lunna
Brae
Muckle Roe
A 970
Voe
Laxo
Whalsay
A 360
Dury Voe
Papa Stour
Aith
SHETLAND
Sandness
M a i n l a n d
A 971
Walls
Tresta
Reawick
Vaila
Lerwick
I. of Noss
Ham **Foula**
Scalloway
Bressay
To Bergen & Hanstolm (Summer Only)
Bressay Sd.
Hamnavoe
West Burra
Cunningsburgh
Cliff Sd.
A 970
A 25
Sandwick
Scousburgh
Mousa
Fitful Head
Tolob
Sumburgh Head
Sumburgh

To Stromness
Stonybreck **Fair Isle**
To Aberdeen

LONDON
Chipping Ongar
Ingatestone
Brentwood
Epping
Waltham Abbey
Cheshunt
Enfield
Potters Bar
Barnet
Chigwell
Abridge
Romford
Ilford
Dagenham
Barking
Rainham
Purfleet
Tilbury
Grays
Thurrock
Orsett
Upminster
Hornchurch
Woodford
Edmonton
Ponders End
New Barnet
Finchley
Hendon
Golders Green
Hampstead
Edgware
Stanmore
Wembley
Harrow
Pinner
Bushey
Watford
Rickmansworth
Chenies
Chesham
Amersham
Chalfont St. Giles
Beaconsfield
Gerrards Cross
Denham
Uxbridge
Northolt
Southall
Ealing
Brentford
Hounslow
Richmond
Twickenham
Kingston
Surbiton
Staines
Colnbrook
Slough
Windsor
Datchet
Egham
Chertsey
Weybridge
Walton
Hampton
Esher
Cobham
Epsom
Ewell
Cheam
Sutton
Mitcham
Croydon
Streatham
Lewisham
Greenwich
Woolwich
Thamesmead
Erith
Bexley
Eltham
Sidcup
Bromley
Chislehurst
Orpington
Farnborough
Keston
Addington
Sanderstead
Warlingham
Purley
Banstead
Caterham
Redhill
Reigate
Leatherhead
Ashtead
Mickleham
Woking
Old Woking
Byfleet
Ripley
Guildford
Horsley
Clandon
Merrow
Bisley
Horsell
Chobham
Ottershaw
Dartford
Swanley
Kingsdown
Eynsford
Farningham
Meopham
Cobham
Wrotham
Sevenoaks
Seal
Otford
Riverhead
Westerham
Brasted
Limpsfield
Godstone
Crockham Hill
Oxted
Hadlow
Mereworth
Borough Gr.
Snodland
Elstree
Radlett
Borehamwood
S. Mimms
M25
M1
M4
M3
M20
M26
M11
A1(M)
North Downs

Index

This index comprises a selection of names and locations of towns and villages based on population, route importance, and postal significance.
The reference number refers to the page, and the letter refers to the section of the map in which the index entry can be found, as divided into **a, b, c,** and **d** thus:

A

Abbey St.Bathans	75b
Abbey Town	65d
Abbotsbury	8c
Aberaeron	25a
Aberargie	81b
Abercarn	24d
Aberchirder	95b
Aberdare	24a
Aberdaron	43c
Aberdeen	96c
Aberdour	81d
Aberdyfi	33c
Aberedw	26a
Aberfeldy	86d
Aberffraw	43b
Abergavenny	24b
Abergele	44b
Abergwynfi	24a
Aberlady	82c
Aberllefenni	33b
Aberlour	94a
Abernethy	81b
Aberporth	22a
Abersoch	43d
Abertillery	24b
Aberystwyth	25b
Abingdon	17b
Abington	73d
Aboyne	88a
Accrington	52c
Acharacle	84c
Acharn	86c
Achavanich	101a
Achiltibuie	97b
Achintree	90b
Achnasheen	91b
Acklington	68a
Acock's Green	36c
Acomb	54b
Acton Turville	16a

Adderbury	29c
Addington	19d
Adwick-le-Street	48a
Ainsdale	51d
Aintree	45b
Aird of Sleat	84a
Airdrie	73b
Airth	81c
Albrighton	35d
Alcester	28a
Aldbrough	56c
Aldeburgh	41d
Alderley Edge	46b
Alderminster	28b
Aldershot	11a
Alexandria	79d
Alford (Grampian)	95d
Alford (Lincs)	50c
Alfreton	48c
Alfriston	12c
Alkham	14a
Allanby	65d
Allenheads	67d
Allesley	28b
Allgreave	47c
Alloa	80d
Almondsbury	15b
Alness	93a
Alnmouth	68a
Alnwick	68a
Alpheton	32a
Alresford	10a
Alrewas	36a
Alston	66d
Alston Cross	28c
Altassmore	99b
Altnaharra	100a
Alton	10b
Altrincham	46b
Alva	81c

Alvanley	46c	Arundel	11c
Alvaston	36b	Ascot	18c
Alvechurch	28a	Asfordby	37b
Alyth	87d	Ash	14a
Amble	68a	Ashbourne	36a
Ambleside	58c	Ashburton	4a
Amersham	18a	Ashby	49b
Amesbury	9b	Ashby de la Zouch	36b
Amlwch	43b	Ashford (Kent)	13b
Ammanford	23b	Ashington	68a
Ampleforth	61d	Ashstead	19c
Ampthill	30c	Ashton Keynes	16b
Amulree	80b	Ashton-under-Lyne	47a
Ancaster	38a	Ashton-in-Makerfield	46a
Ancroft	76c	Askham	57d
Andover	9b	Aspatria	65d
Andoversford	28c	Aston	48a
Annan	65d	Atherstone	36d
Annbank	72c	Atherton	46a
Anstruther	82b	Attleborough	42a
Appleby	58b	Atwick	56a
Applecross	90a	Atworth	16c
Appledore (Devon)	5b	Auchencairn	64d
Appledore (Kent)	13d	Auchentiber	72a
Arbroath	88c	Auchinblae	88a
Archiestown	94a	Auchindown	95a
Ardarroch	90c	Auchinleck	73c
Ardbeg	69b	Auchterarder	81b
Ardcharnich	97c	Auchtermuchty	82a
Ardentinny	79d	Aultbea	97a
Ardeonaig	80a	Aviemore	93d
Ardersier	93b	Avoch	93a
Ardfern	78a	Avonmouth	15b
Ardgay	99c	Axbridge	15c
Ardlui	79b	Axminster	7d
Ardlussa	77d	Aylesbury	30c
Ardmair	97b	Aylesham	14a
Ardminish	70a	Aylsham	40a
Ardrishaig	78c	Aynho	29d
Ardrossan	71b	Ayr	71d
Ardtalla	69b	Aysgarth	59d
Arduaine	78a	Ayton	76a
Arinagour	83c		
Arisaig	84a	**B**	
Armadale (Skye)	84a		
Armadale (Highland)	100b	Backaland	101d
Arncliffe	52b	Bacup	52d
Arnesby	37c	Badcall	98c
Arnisdale	90d	Badluachrach	97a
Arnprior	80c	Bagby	61d
Arnside	51b	Bagshot	18c
Arrochar	79d	Bakewell	47d
Arthog	33a	Bala	44d

Balallan	103b	Basingstoke	17d
Balbair	93a	Baslow	47d
Balbeggie	81b	Bath	15d
Balcombe	12a	Bathgate	73b
Baldock	30d	Batley	54c
Balerno	74a	Battle	13c
Balfour	101c	Battlefield	35a
Balintore	93b	Baumber	50c
Ballachulish	85c	Bawtry	48b
Ballantrae	63a	Baynards Green	29d
Ballater	87b	Beaconsfield	18a
Ballaugh	51c	Beadnell	76d
Ballinluig	86d	Beal	76c
Ballygrant	69b	Beaminster	8c
Balmaha	79d	Beattock	65b
Balmullo	82a	Beaulieu	9d
Balsham	31b	Beauly	92a
Baltasound	104b	Beaumaris	44a
Bamber Bridge	52c	Bebington	45b
Bamburgh	76d	Beccles	42c
Bampton	7a	Beckingham	49a
Banbury	29c	Bedale	60c
Banchory	28a	Bedford	30b
Banff	95b	Bedlington	68c
Bangor	44a	Bedworth	36d
Bannockburn	81c	Beer	7d
Banstead	19c	Beeston	37a
Barbaraville	93b	Beith	71b
Barcaldine	79a	Belford	76d
Bardon Mill	67d	Bellingham	67b
Bardsea	51b	Bellochantuy	70c
Bargoed	24b	Bellshill	73a
Bargrennan	63b	Belmont	52c
Barking	19b	Belper	48c
Barlborough	48c	Belsay	68a
Barmouth	33a	Bembridge	10c
Barnard Castle	60a	Benson	17b
Barnet	19a	Bentley	48a
Barnoldswick	53a	Bere Regis	8d
Barnsley	48a	Berkeley	15b
Barnstaple	6a	Berkhamsted	18a
Barr	63b	Bernisdale	89b
Barrhead	72a	Berriedale	99b
Barrhill	63b	Berryhillock	95b
Barrow	56c	Berwick-upon-Tweed	76a
Barrow-in-Furness	51a	Bethesda	44a
Barry	24d	Bettyhill	100b
Barton (Humberside)	56c	Betws-y-Coed	44b
Barton (Bedfordshire)	30c	Beulah	26a
Barton Mills	31b	Beverley	56c
Barvas	103b	Bewdley	27b
Baschurch	34b	Bexhill-on-Sea	13d
Basildon	20a	Bexley	19b

Bicester	29d
Bickley Moss	46c
Biddendon	13d
Biddulph	47c
Bideford	5b
Bidford	28a
Bigbury on Sea	3d
Biggar	74c
Biggleswade	30b
Bilbister	101b
Billericay	20a
Billesdon	37d
Billingborough	38a
Billingshurst	11b
Bilston	35d
Bingham	37b
Bingley	53d
Binley	29a
Birchington	14b
Birdlip	28c
Birgham	75d
Birkenhead	45b
Birmingham	36c
Birnam	87c
Birsay	101d
Birtley	68c
Bishop Auckland	60a
Bishopbriggs	73a
Bishop Burton	55d
Bishops Castle	34c
Bishop's Caundle	8a
Bishop's Cleeve	28c
Bishops Lydeard	7b
Bishop's Stortford	31c
Bishops Waltham	10a
Bisley	18c
Bitterne	10a
Blaby	37c
Blackbrook	35b
Blackburn	52c
Blackford	81a
Blackmoor Gate	6a
Blackness	81d
Blackpool	51d
Blackwaterfoot	70c
Blackwood (S'clyde)	73b
Blackwood (Gwent)	24d
Bladnoch	64c
Blaenau Ffestiniog	44c
Blaenavon	24b
Blaenporth	22a
Blaenrhondda	24a
Blagdon (Avon)	15d
Blagdon (Somerset)	7b
Blair Atholl	86d
Blairgowrie	87c
Blakeney (Norfolk)	40a
Blakeney (Glos)	15b
Blakenham	32b
Blanchland	67d
Blandford Forum	8b
Blankney	49d
Blantyre	73a
Blaydon	68c
Blean	14a
Bletchingley	12a
Blewbury	17b
Blindley Heath	12a
Blofield	42c
Bloxwich	36c
Blubberhouses	53b
Blyth (Northumberland)	68a
Blyth Bridge	74a
Blythburgh	41d
Blyton	49a
Boat of Garton	93d
Bodfari	45c
Bodmin	2b
Bognor Regis	11c
Boldon	68d
Boldre	9d
Bollington	47a
Bolton	46a
Bolventor	2b
Bonar Bridge	99a
Boncath	22a
Bonchester Bridge	75d
Bo'ness	81d
Bonhill	79d
Bonnyrigg	74b
Boothby Pagnell	38a
Bootle (Cumbria)	57d
Bootle (Merseyside)	45b
Boreland	65b
Borough Green	20c
Boroughbridge	54a
Borrowdale	57b
Borth	33c
Borve	103b
Boscastle	5c
Bosley	47c
Boston	50c
Botesdale	41b
Bothwell	73a
Botley (Oxon)	17b
Botley (Hants)	10a

Bourne	38a	Bridge of Weir	71b
Bournemouth	9c	Bridgend (Strathclyde)	69a
Bovey Tracey	4a	Bridgend (Mid Glamorgan)	24c
Bow	4a	Bridgnorth	35d
Bow Street	33c	Bridgwater	7b
Bowes	59b	Bridlington	56a
Bowland Bridge	58c	Bridport	8c
Bowling	80c	Brierley Hill	35d
Bowmore	69a	Brigg	49b
Bowness	58c	Brighouse	53d
Box	16c	Brighstone	10c
Bracadale	89d	Brightling	13c
Bracebridge	49d	Brightlingsea	32d
Brackley	29d	Brighton	12c
Bracknell	18c	Brinkley	31b
Braco	80b	Brinkworth	16a
Bradfield	17d	Brinyan	101d
Bradford	53d	Brisley	40a
Bradford-on-Avon	16c	Bristol	15b
Bradwell on Sea	20b	Briton Ferry	23d
Braemar	87a	Brixham	4c
Brailsford	36a	Brixworth	29b
Braintree	31d	Broad Chalke	9a
Bramdean	10a	Broad Clyst	7c
Bramham	54c	Broad Haven	21d
Bramley	11b	Broad Hinton	16b
Brampton (Cambs)	30b	Broadford	90c
Brampton (Cumbria)	66c	Broadstairs	14b
Brancaster	39b	Broadway	28d
Brancepeth	60a	Broadwey	8c
Brandesburton	56a	Broadwindsor	7d
Brandon (Durham)	60a	Brockenhurst	9d
Brandon (Suffolk)	39d	Brodick	70b
Branston	49d	Bromborough	45b
Brant Broughton	49d	Bromley	19d
Braunton	5b	Brompton	62d
Brayford	6a	Bromsgrove	28a
Breage	1d	Bromyard	27b
Breakish	90c	Bronnant	25b
Bream	15b	Brookland	13d
Brechin	88c	Brora	99b
Brecon	24a	Broseley	35c
Brede	13d	Brotton	62a
Bredhurst	20c	Brough	58b
Brentford	19a	Broughton (Borders)	74c
Brentwood	19b	Broughton (Cumbria)	57d
Brenzett	13d	Brownhills	36c
Bridge of Alford	95d	Broxburn	74a
Bridge of Allan	81c	Bruton	8a
Bridge of Cally	87c	Bryn-amman	25d
Bridge of Earn	81b	Bryn-crug	33c
Bridge of Gairn	87b	Bryneglwys	45c
Bridge of Orchy	85d	Brynmawr	24b

Bubwith	55d
Buckden	30b
Buckfastleigh	4c
Buckhaven	82c
Buckie	94b
Buckingham	29d
Buckley	45d
Bucks Green	11b
Bucksburn	88b
Bude	5c
Budleigh Salterton	7c
Builth Wells	26a
Bulwick	38c
Bunessan	77a
Bungay	42c
Bunny	37a
Buntingford	31c
Bures	32c
Burford	28d
Burgess Hill	12c
Burgh le Marsh	50d
Burghead	94a
Burley	53c
Burnham	15c
Burnham Market	39b
Burnham on Crouch	20b
Burnhaven	96b
Burniston	62d
Burnley	52d
Burnmouth	76a
Burnopfield	68c
Burnsall	53b
Burntisland	82c
Burravoe	104b
Burry Port	22d
Burscough Bridge	45b
Burslem	46d
Burton	49d
Burton Agnes	56a
Burton Leonard	54a
Burton in Kendal	58c
Burton in Lonsdale	52a
Burton upon Trent	36a
Burwash	13c
Burwell (Cambs)	31b
Burwell (Lincs)	50a
Burwick	101c
Bury	46b
Bury St Edmonds	32a
Buttermere	57b
Buttington	34a
Buxton	47d
Byfleet	18d
Byrness	66b
Bythorne	30a

C

Cadbury	4a
Cadnam	9b
Caenby Corner	49b
Caerleon	15a
Caernarfon	43b
Caerphilly	24d
Caersws	34c
Caerwent	15a
Cairnbaan	78c
Cairnryan	63a
Caister-on-Sea	42d
Caistor	49b
Caldbeck	66c
Caldecott	37d
Calder Bridge	57c
Caldercruix	72b
Caldicot	15b
Caldwell	60a
Calgary	83d
Callander	80a
Callanish	103b
Callington	3b
Calne	16c
Calveley	46c
Calver	47d
Camberley	18c
Camborne	1d
Cambridge	31a
Camelford	5c
Cammachmore	88b
Campbeltown	70c
Camptown	67a
Cannich	92c
Cannington	7b
Cannock	35d
Canonbie	66a
Canterbury	14a
Canvey	20a
Capel	11b
Capenhurst	45d
Capplegill	74c
Caputh	87c
Carbis Bay	1d
Carbost	89b
Cardiff	24d
Cardigan	22a
Carinish	103c
Carisbrooke	10c

Carlisle	66c	Checkley	36a
Carlops	74a	Cheddar	15c
Carlton on Trent	48d	Chelmsford	20a
Carluke	73b	Cheltenham	28c
Carmarthen	22b	Chepstow	15b
Carnforth	51b	Cheriton	10a
Carno	33d	Chertsey	18d
Carnoustie	82b	Chesham	18b
Carnwath	73b	Cheshunt	19b
Carradale	70a	Chessell	10c
Carrbridge	93d	Chester	45d
Carrick Castle	78d	Chester-le-Street	68c
Carronbridge	65a	Chesterfield	48c
Carsphairn	64a	Chew Stoke	15d
Carstairs	73b	Chicheley	30a
Carter Bar	67a	Chichester	11c
Casterton	58c	Chicklade	9a
Castlebay	103a	Chiddingfold	11a
Castle Cary	98a	Chideock	7d
Castle Douglas	64d	Chigwell	19b
Castleford	54c	Chilham	14a
Castle Hedingham	32c	Chillingham	76c
Castle Kennedy	63d	Chilton Foliat	17c
Castle Rising	39b	Chinnor	18a
Castleside	68c	Chippenham	16a
Castleton (Derbys)	47b	Chipping Camden	28d
Castleton (N.Yorks)	62b	Chipping Norton	28d
Castletown	51c	Chipping Ongar	19b
Caterham	19a	Chipping Sodbury	15b
Catterick	60c	Chirnside	76a
Cavendish	32a	Chiseldon	16b
Cawdor	93b	Chiselhurst	19d
Caxton	31a	Chobham	18c
Cemaes Bay	43b	Chorley	52c
Ceres	82a	Christchurch	9d
Cerne Abbas	8c	Chryston	72b
Chagford	4a	Chudleigh	4a
Chale	10c	Chulmleigh	6c
Chalfont St. Giles	18a	Church Stretton	34d
Chandler's Ford	10a	Churchill	15c
Chapel Allerton	54c	Churston Ferrers	4c
Chapel en le Frith	47b	Cinderford	27d
Chapel St.Leonards	50d	Cirencester	16a
Chard	7b	Clachnaharry	92b
Charlbury	29c	Clackmannan	80d
Charlton Kings	28c	Clacton-on-Sea	32d
Charlwood	11b	Clanfield	10b
Charmouth	7d	Claonaig	70a
Chatham	20c	Clapham	52a
Chatteris	38d	Clarencefield	65d
Chatton	76c	Clashmore	99a
Cheadle (Staffs)	36a	Clashnessie	98a
Cheadle (Grtr Manchester)	46b	Clawton	5d

Clay Cross	48c	Connel	78a
Claydon	41a	Conon Bridge	92a
Clayton-le-Moors	52d	Consett	68c
Cleator	57a	Contin	92a
Cleehill	27b	Conwy	44a
Cleethorpes	50a	Conwyl Elfed	22a
Cleobury Mortimer	27b	Cooden	13c
Clevedon	15c	Cookham	18a
Cleveleys	51d	Coolham	11b
Clitheroe	52c	Coombe Bissett	9b
Cloughton	62d	Coombe Martin	6c
Clova	87b	Copplestone	6c
Clovelly	5b	Corbridge	67d
Clovenfords	75c	Corby	37d
Clun	34c	Corfe Castle	9c
Clydebank	72a	Corhampton	10a
Clynder	79d	Cornhill (Grampian)	95b
Clyst Honiton	7c	Cornhill on Tweed	76c
Coalville	36b	Cornwood	3d
Coatbridge	73a	Corpach	85a
Cobham (Surrey)	18d	Corran	84d
Cobham (Kent)	20c	Corrie Common	65b
Cockburnspath	75b	Corringham	49a
Cockenzie	82c	Corsham	16c
Cockermouth	57b	Corston	16a
Codicote	30d	Corwen	34a
Coggleshall	32c	Cosham	10a
Colchester	32c	Coshieville	86c
Cold Ashton	15d	Cotherstone	59b
Coldingham	76a	Cottenham	31a
Cold Norton	20a	Cottingham	56c
Coldstream	76c	Coupar Angus	87d
Coleford (Glos)	15b	Cove	79d
Coleshill	36c	Coventry	29a
Colintraive	78d	Coverack	2c
Collieston	96d	Cowbridge	24c
Collingham (W.Yorks)	54a	Cowdenbeath	81d
Collingham (Notts)	49c	Cowes	10c
Colmonell	63b	Cowfold	11b
Colnbrook	18b	Coxhoe	61a
Colne	52d	Coychurch	24c
Colpy	95d	Crackleybank	35b
Colsterworth	37b	Craigellachie	94b
Coltishall	42b	Craighouse	69b
Colwyn Bay	44b	Craignure	78a
Colyford	7d	Craigton	87d
Comrie	80b	Crail	82b
Congleton	46d	Cramlington	68c
Congresbury	15c	Cranborne	9a
Coningsby	50c	Cranbrook	13d
Conisbrough	48a	Cranford St.John	30a
Coniston	57d	Cranleigh	11b
Connah's Quay	45d	Cranswick	56a

Crathorne	61d
Craven Arms	34d
Crawford	73d
Crawfordjohn	73d
Crawley	11b
Cray	24a
Creagorry	103c
Credenhill	27c
Crediton	4a
Creetown	64c
Cresselly	21d
Crewe	46c
Crewkerne	7b
Crianlarich	79b
Cribyn	25a
Criccieth	43d
Crickhowell	26d
Cricklade	16b
Crieff	80b
Crinan	78c
Crockernwell	4a
Crockham Hill	12a
Croft	61c
Cromarty	93b
Cromdale	94c
Cromer	40b
Cromford	48a
Crook	60a
Crosby (Merseyside)	45b
Crosby (I.of W.)	51c
Crosby Ravensworth	58b
Croshills	53b
Cross Hands	23b
Cross-Keys	24d
Crossaig	70a
Crosshill	71d
Crowborough	12a
Crowcombe	7a
Crowland	38a
Crowle	55d
Crowthorne	18c
Croxton Kerrial	37b
Croydon	19d
Cruden Bay	96d
Crudgington	35a
Crudwell	16a
Crymmych	22a
Crynant	23b
Cuckfield	12a
Cudworth	48a
Culgaith	59a
Culkein	98a
Cullen	95b
Cullompton	7a
Culmstock	7a
Culross	81d
Cults	88b
Cumbernauld	73b
Cuminestown	96a
Cumnock	72c
Cunningsburgh	104d
Cupar	82a
Currie	74a
Cury Cross	1d
Cwmbran	15a

D

Dagenham	19b
Dalbeattie	64d
Dale	21d
Daliburgh	103c
Dalkeith	74b
Dallas	94a
Dalleagles	72c
Dalmally	78b
Dalmellington	72c
Dalry (D & G)	64a
Dalry (S'clyde)	71b
Dalsetter	104b
Dalton	51b
Dalwhinnie	86a
Danbury	20a
Daresbury	46a
Darfield	48a
Darlington	60a
Dartford	19b
Dartmeet	4a
Dartmouth	4c
Darvel	72a
Darwen	52c
Dava	94c
Daventry	29b
Davidstow	5c
Daviot	93b
Dawley	35d
Dawlish	4b
Deal	14b
Debenham	41b
Deddington	29c
Deeping St.Nicholas	38a
Denbigh	45c
Denby Dale	47b
Denham	18b
Denholm	75d
Dennington	41b

Denny	80d
Denton	47a
Derby	36b
Dereham	40a
Dersingham	39b
Dervaig	83d
Deskford	95b
Devizes	16c
Devonport	3d
Dewsbury	54c
Diabaig	90a
Dicker	12c
Didcot	17b
Didmarton	16a
Dingwall	92a
Dinnet	87b
Dirleton	82d
Diss	32b
Distington	57a
Ditton Priors	35c
Docking	39b
Docklow	27b
Doddington	38d
Dolbenmaen	43d
Dolgellau	33a
Dollar	81d
Dolphinton	74a
Dolwyddelan	44c
Doncaster	48b
Donington (Lincs)	38a
Dorchester (Dorset)	8c
Dorchester (Oxon)	17b
Dores	93c
Dorking	11b
Dornie	90d
Dornoch	99a
Dorrington	34d
Douglas (Strathclyde)	73d
Douglas (I.of M.)	51c
Dounby	101d
Doune	80d
Dounreay	100d
Dover	14b
Dowally	86d
Downham Market	39c
Downton	9b
Draycott	36a
Drayton	42b
Drem	82d
Droitwich	28a
Dronfield	48a
Drumbeg	98a
Drummore	63d
Drumnadrochit	92c
Drumnaich	80a
Drynoch	89d
Duddo	76c
Dudley	35d
Duffield	36b
Dufftown	95a
Duffus	94a
Duirnish	90c
Dulnain Bridge	94c
Dulverton	6b
Dumbarton	79d
Dumfries	65a
Dunbar	75b
Dunbeath	100b
Dunblane	80b
Dunbridge	9b
Dundee	82a
Dundonald	72a
Dundrennan	64d
Dunfermline	81d
Dunholme	49b
Dunkeld	86d
Dunlop	72a
Dunnet	101b
Dunning	81b
Dunoon	78d
Duns	75b
Dunstable	30c
Dunster	7a
Dunsyre	74a
Dunvegan	89a
Dunwich	41d
Durham	60a
Durness	98d
Dursley	16a
Durston	7b
Durweston	8b
Duthil	93d
Dyce	96c
Dykehead	87d
Dymchurch	14c
Dymock	27d
Dysart	82c
E	
Eaglesham	73a
Eaglesham	72a
Earby	53a
Earls Colne	32c
Earlston	75d
Easdale	78a

Easebourne	11a	Eltham	19d
Easington	68d	Elton	38c
East Barkwith	50a	Elvanfoot	73d
East Bridgford	37b	Elvington	55a
Eastbourne	12d	Elworthy	7a
East Cowes	10c	Ely	31b
Eastchurch	20d	Embleton	76d
Eastdean	12d	Emsworth	10b
East Grinstead	12a	Enfield	19b
East Hoathley	12c	Epping	19b
East Horsley	11b	Epsom	19c
Easthampstead	18c	Epworth	49a
Easthampton	18c	Eriboll	98d
East Kilbride	72b	Errogie	92c
Eastleigh	10a	Erwood	26c
East Linton	82d	Esher	18d
East Lulworth	8d	Etal	76c
East Markham	49c	Ettington	28b
East Retford	48b	Ettrickbridge End	75c
Eastriggs	65d	Evanton	92a
Eastry	14b	Evelix	99a
East Wemyss	82c	Evercreech	8a
Eastwood	48c	Everingham	55d
Eaton Socon	30b	Evesham	28c
Ebbw Vale	24b	Ewenny	24c
Ebchester	68c	Ewhurst	11b
Ecclefechan	65b	Exbourne	3b
Eccleshall	35b	Exeter	4b
Echt	96c	Exford	6b
Eckington	48a	Exminster	4a
Edderton	99a	Exmouth	4b
Eddlestone	74a	Eye	41b
Edenbridge	12a	Eyemouth	76a
Edgcumbe	1d	Eynsford	19d
Edgware	19a	Eynsham	17b
Edinbane	89b		
Edinburgh	74a	**F**	
Edzell	88c		
Egham	18d	Fairford	16b
Eglingham	76d	Fairlie	71b
Egremont	57a	Fakenham	39b
Eilean Iarmain	90c	Falkirk	80d
Elgin	94a	Falkland	82a
Elgol	89d	Falmer	12c
Elie	82c	Falmouth	2c
Elland	53d	Falstone	66b
Ellesmere	34b	Fangfoss	55b
Ellesmere Port	45b	Fareham	10a
Ellon	96c	Faringdon	17a
Elphin	97d	Farnborough (London)	19d
Elrick	96c	Farnborough (Hants)	11a
Elstow	30a	Farndon	45d
Elstree	19a	Farnham	11a

Farnham Royal	18a
Farnworth	46a
Faversham	13b
Fawley	10c
Fazeley	36c
Fearn	93b
Fearnan	86c
Featherstone	54c
Felbridge	12a
Felixstowe	41c
Felling	68c
Felpham	11c
Felton	68a
Feltwell	39d
Fenstanton	31a
Fenwick	72a
Feolin	69b
Ferndown	9c
Fernhurst	11a
Ferrybridge	54c
Ferryhill	60a
Ferryside	22d
Fettercairn	88a
Ffestiniog	44c
Ffostrasol	22b
Filby	42d
Filey	56a
Filton	15b
Finborough	41b
Finchingfield	31d
Finchley	19a
Findhorn	94a
Findochty	95b
Findon	11d
Finedon	30a
Finnart	79d
Finstown	101c
Fionnphort	77a
Fishbourne	10c
Fishguard	21b
Fishnish	84c
Fiskavaig	89d
Fittleworth	11b
Flamborough	56a
Flax Bourton	15d
Fleet	18c
Fleetwood	51b
Flimby	57a
Flimwell	13c
Flint	45d
Flitsham	39b
Flyford Flavell	28a
Folkestone	14c
Folkingham	38a
Fontmell Magna	8b
Ford	76c
Fordham	31b
Fordingbridge	9b
Forest Row	12a
Forfar	87d
Formby	45b
Fornham St.Martin	32a
Forres	94a
Fort Augustus	92c
Fort George	93b
Fort William	85a
Fortinghall	86c
Fortrose	93b
Fortuneswell	8c
Four Oaks	36c
Fovant	9a
Fowey	2b
Foxholes	56a
Foyers	92c
Fraddon	2a
Framlingham	41b
Frant	13c
Fraserburgh	96b
Freshwater	9d
Fressingfield	41b
Freswick	101b
Fridaythorpe	55b
Frinton	32d
Friockheim	88c
Frodsham	46a
Frome	16c
Frosterley	60a
Fulford	55a
Fulwood	52c
Fyfield	19b
Fyvie	96c

G

Gaerwen	43b
Gailey	35b
Gainford	60a
Gainsborough	49a
Gairloch	90a
Gairlochy	85a
Gairlogie	96c
Galashiels	75c
Galgate	51b
Galson	103b
Galston	72a
Gardenstown	96a

Garforth	54c
Gargrave	53a
Garlieston	64c
Garlogie	88b
Garmouth	94b
Garstang	51b
Garston	45b
Garth (Powys)	26a
Garth (Mid Glam)	24c
Gartmore	80c
Gartocharn	79d
Garvald	82d
Garve	92a
Garynahine	103b
Gatehouse of Fleet	64c
Gateshead	68c
Geddington	37d
Gedney Drove End	39a
George Nympton	6a
Gerrards Cross	18a
Giffnock	73a
Gifford	82d
Gilfach Goch	24c
Gillingham (Dorset)	8b
Gillingham (Kent)	20c
Gills	101b
Gilwern	26d
Girtford	30b
Girvan	63b
Gisburn	53a
Glamis	87d
Glasgow	73a
Glastonbury	8a
Glenbarr	70c
Glenbrittle	89d
Glencarse	81b
Glencoe	85c
Glendevon	81b
Glenelg	90c
Glenfinnan	84b
Glenluce	63d
Glenrothes	82c
Glossop	47b
Gloucester	28c
Glyn Neath	24a
Glyncorrwg	24a
Glyntaw	23b
Gnoshall	35b
Goathland	62c
Godalming	11a
Godmanchester	30b
Godshill (Hants)	9b
Godshill (I. of W.)	10c
Godstone	12a
Goginan	33c
Golders Green	19a
Golspie	99d
Goodwick	21b
Goole	55d
Gordonstoun	94a
Gorebridge	74b
Goring	17b
Gorleston	42c
Gosfield	32c
Gosforth	68c
Gosport	10c
Goudhurst	13d
Gourock	79d
Govan	73a
Gramisdale	103c
Grampound	2a
Grange (Cumbria)	51b
Grangemouth	81c
Grantham	37b
Granthouse	76a
Grantown-on-Spey	94c
Grasmere	57b
Grassington	53b
Gravesend	20a
Grayrigg	58c
Great Ayton	61d
Great Baddow	20a
Great Bradfield	31d
Great Chart	13b
Great Chesterford	31c
Great Driffield	56a
Great Dunmow	31d
Great Harwood	52c
Great Malvern	27b
Great Missenden	18a
Great Musgrave	59b
Great Offley	30d
Great Smeaton	60d
Greatstone-on-Sea	14c
Great Torrington	5b
Great Weldon	37d
Great Witley	27b
Great Yarmouth	42d
Green Hammerton	54a
Greenfield	45a
Greenhead	66d
Greenlaw	75d
Greenloaning	80b
Greenock	79d
Greenodd	57d
Greenwich	19b

Gretna	65d	Haroldswick	104b
Gretna Green	65d	Harpenden	30d
Greystoke	58a	Harrietsham	20c
Grimsby	50a	Harrogate	54a
Gringley on the Hill	49a	Harrow	18b
Grinton	60c	Hart	61b
Grizebeck	57d	Hartfield	12a
Groby	37c	Hartland	5b
Groombridge	12a	Hartlebury	28a
Gruinard	97a	Hartlepool	60b
Gruinart	69a	Hartley Wintney	18c
Guildford	11b	Harwell	17b
Guisborough	61b	Harwich	32d
Guiseley	53d	Hascombe	11a
Gullane	82c	Haslemere	11a
Gunnislake	3b	Haslingden	52c
Guyhirn	38d	Hastings	13d
Gwbert-on-Sea	22a	Hatfield (Herts)	19a
		Hatfield (S.Yorks)	48b
H		Hatherleigh	6c
		Hathersage	47b
Haddenham	31a	Havant	10b
Haddington	75a	Haverfordwest	21d
Hadleigh (Suffolk)	32c	Haverhill	31b
Hadleigh (Essex)	20a	Hawes	59d
Hailsham	12d	Hawick	75c
Hale	46b	Hawkhurst	13d
Halesowen	28a	Hawkshead	57d
Halesworth	40d	Haworth	53d
Halford	28b	Haxey	49a
Halifax	53d	Hay-on-Wye	26d
Halkirk	100d	Haydon Bridge	67d
Halland	12c	Hayle	1d
Halloughton	48d	Haytor Vale	4a
Hallsands	4c	Haywards Heath	12a
Halstead	32c	Heacham	39b
Halton Gill	52b	Headcorn	13b
Haltwhistle	66d	Heanor	36b
Halwell	4c	Heathfield	13c
Ham Street	13d	Hebden Bridge	53d
Hamble	10a	Heckfield	18c
Hambledon	10a	Heckington	38a
Hamilton	73a	Heckmondwike	53d
Hampstead	19a	Heddon on the Wall	68c
Hampton	18d	Hedon	56c
Handsworth (Yorks)	48a	Heiton	75d
Hanley	46d	Helensburgh	79d
Harbottle	67b	Helmsdale	99b
Hardwicke	27d	Helmsley	61d
Harlech	44c	Helsby	46a
Harleston	42a	Helston	1d
Harlow	19b	Hemel Hempstead	18b
Harmerhill	34b	Hemsby	42d

Hendon	19a
Henfield	11d
Henley in Arden	28b
Henley-on-Thames	18a
Henlow	30d
Henstridge	8b
Hereford	27c
Hermitage	17d
Herne	14a
Herne Bay	14a
Hertford	19b
Hessle	56c
Heswall	45b
Hethersett	42a
Hetton le Hole	68d
Hexham	67d
Heysham	51b
Heywood	46b
Hibaldstow	49b
High Bentham	52a
Highclere	17c
High Hampton	5d
High Hawsker	62c
High Hesket	58a
High Wycombe	18a
Highworth	16b
Hilborough	39d
Hilderthorpe	56a
Hillswick	104a
Hinckley	36d
Hinderwell	62a
Hindhead	11a
Hindley	46a
Hintlesham	32b
Hirwaun	24a
Histon	31a
Hitchin	30d
Hobkirk	75d
Hockering	42b
Hoddesdon	19a
Hodnet	35a
Holbeach	38b
Holkham	39b
Holme (Cumbria)	58c
Holme (Humberside)	55d
Holmes Chapel	46d
Holmfirth	47b
Holsworthy	3a
Holt	40a
Holyhead	43b
Holytown	73b
Holywell	45c
Homersfield	42a

Honington	32a
Honiton	7d
Hook (Hants)	18c
Hope Bowdler	34d
Hope under Dinmore	27a
Horbury	54c
Horley	12a
Horncastle	50c
Horndean	10b
Hornden	20a
Horns Cross	5b
Hornsea	56a
Horsforth	54c
Horsham	11b
Horton in Ribblesdale	52b
Horwich	46a
Houghton-le-Spring	68d
Hounslow	18d
Hove	12c
Hovingham	55a
Howden	55d
Hownam	75d
Hoxne	41b
Hoylake	45b
Hucknall	48c
Huddersfield	53d
Huggate	55b
Hull	56c
Humberstone	50a
Huna	101b
Hunford	72a
Hungerford	17c
Hunmanby	56a
Hunstanton	39b
Huntingdon	30b
Huntley	95b
Hurstbourne Tarrant	17c
Hurstmonceux	13c
Hurstpierpoint	12c
Hurworth	61a
Husbands Bosworth	37c
Hutton Rudby	61d
Hyde	47a
Hythe (Kent)	14c
Hythe (Hants)	10a

I

Ibsley	9b
Ibstock	36b
Ilchester	8a
Ilfracombe	6a
Ilkestone	36b

Ilkley	53d	Jarrow	68d
Ilminster	7b	Jedburgh	75d
Immingham	56c	John o' Groats	101b
Inchbare	88c	Johnston	21d
Inchnadamph	97d	Johnstone	72a
Inchture	82a		
Indian Queens	2a	**K**	
Inellan	79d		
Ingatestone	20a	Kames	78d
Ingbirchworth	47b	Kegworth	37a
Ingleton	52a	Keighley	53d
Ingoldmells	50d	Keills	77d
Innerleithen	74d	Keiss	101b
Insch	95d	Keith	95b
Insh	86a	Keld	59d
Inveralligin	90a	Kelham	49c
Inverallochy	96b	Kellybray	2a
Inveraray	78b	Kelmarsh	29b
Inverbeg	79d	Kelsall	46c
Inverbervie	88c	Kelso	75d
Inverewe	97a	Kelty	81d
Inverey	87a	Kelvedon	32c
Inverfarigaig	92c	Kemnay	96c
Invergarry	85b	Kempston	30a
Invergordon	93b	Kendal	58c
Inverinate	91c	Kenilworth	28b
Inverkeilor	88c	Kenmore	86c
Inverkeithing	81d	Kenn	15c
Inverkip	71b	Kennacraig	70a
Inverkirkaig	97b	Kenninghall	42a
Invermoriston	92c	Kessingland	42c
Inverness	93a	Kessock	92b
Inversanda	84d	Keston	19d
Invershiel	90d	Keswick	57b
Invershin	99a	Kettering	30a
Inversnaid	79b	Kettlebridge	82a
Inverurie	96c	Kettlewell	53b
Ipswich	32b	Keynsham	15d
Irlam	46a	Kibworth Harcourt	37d
Ironbridge	35c	Kidderminster	28a
Irthlingborough	30a	Kidlington	29c
Irvine	71b	Kidsgrove	47b
Isbister	104a	Kidwelly	22d
Isle of Whithorn	64c	Kilbarchan	72a
Isleham	31b	Kilberry	70a
Itchen	10a	Kilbirnie	71b
Itchen Stoke	10a	Kilburn	61d
Ivybridge	3d	Kilchattan	71b
Ivychurch	14d	Kilchenzie	70c
		Kilchoan	83d
J		Kilchrenan	78b
		Kilconquhar	82a
Jamestown	79d	Kilcreggan	79d

Kildonan	99d	Kippford	65c
Kilfinan	78c	Kirby Hill	54a
Kilkhampton	5d	Kirby Malzeard	53b
Killean	70a	Kirkaldy	82c
Killimster	101b	Kirkbampton	65d
Killin	80a	Kirkbean	65c
Killingworth	68c	Kirkbride	65d
Kilmalcom	71b	Kirkby	45b
Kilmaluag	89b	Kirkby Lonsdale	58c
Kilmarnock	72a	Kirkbymoorside	62c
Kilmartin	78c	Kirkby Stephen	59b
Kilmaurs	72a	Kirkcolm	63a
Kilmelford	78a	Kirkconnel	72d
Kilmichael	78c	Kirk Deighton	54a
Kilmorach	92a	Kirkfieldbank	73b
Kilmory	78c	Kirkham	51d
Kilmun	79d	Kirkliston	74a
Kilninver	78a	Kirkmichael	87c
Kilnsea	56d	Kirknewton	76c
Kilrenny	82b	Kirkoswald	71d
Kilsby	29b	Kirkpatrick Fleming	65d
Kilwinning	71b	Kirkudbright	64d
Kimberley	42a	Kirkwall	101d
Kinbrace	100c	Kirriemuir	87d
Kincardine	81d	Kirton (Humberside)	49b
Kincardine O'Neil	88a	Kirton (Lincs)	38b
Kincraig	86b	Knaresborough	54a
Kinghorn	82c	Knarsdale	66d
Kingsbarns	82b	Knighton	26b
Kingsbridge	4c	Knockandhu	94c
Kingsclere	17d	Knottingley	54c
Kingsdown	19d	Knutsford	46b
Kingsgate	14b	Kyle of Lochalsh	90c
King's Heath	36c	Kyleakin	90c
King's Langley	18b	Kylerhea	90c
King's Lynn	39a	Kylestrome	98c
Kings Norton	28a		
Kings Somborne	9b	**L**	
Kingsteignton	4a		
Kingston Bagpuize	17a	Laceby	50a
Kingston upon Thames	18d	Lacock	16c
Kingswear	4c	Ladbroke	29a
Kingussie	86a	Ladybank	82a
Kinlochbervie	98d	Lagg	77d
Kinlochewe	90b	Laggan Bridge	86a
Kinloch Hourn	84b	Laide	97a
Kinlochleven	85c	Lairg	99a
Kinlochmoidart	84a	Lakenheath	39d
Kinloch Rannoch	86c	Lamberhurst	13c
Kinloss	94a	Lambourn	17a
Kinross	81b	Lamlash	70d
Kintore	96c	Lampeter	25b
Kippax	54c	Lamphey	21d

Lanark	73b	Leslie	82a
Lancaster	51b	Lesmahagow	73b
Lanchester	68c	Letchworth	30d
Landford	9b	Letheringsett	40a
Lands End	1c	Leuchars	82a
Lane End	18a	Leven	82c
Langholm	66a	Leven	56c
Langport	7b	Leverburgh	103c
Langtoft	56a	Lewes	12c
Lanivet	2a	Lewisham	19b
Lapford	6c	Leyburn	60c
Larbert	81c	Leyland	52c
Largo	82a	Leysdown	20d
Largo Ward	82a	Lhanbryde	94b
Largs	71b	Libberton	73b
Larkhall	73b	Lichfield	36a
Larling	40c	Lifton	3b
Lastingham	62c	Lilliesleaf	75c
Latheron	101a	Limpsfield	12a
Lauder	75a	Lincoln	49d
Laugharne	22c	Lindores	82a
Laughton	12c	Lingdale	62a
Launceston	3a	Linlithgow	73b
Laurencekirk	88a	Linslade	30c
Laurieston	64c	Lintmill	95b
Lavenham	32a	Linton	31b
Lawers	86c	Linwood	72a
Lawton	46d	Liphook	10b
Laxey	51c	Liskeard	3c
Lazonby	58a	Liss	10b
Leadburn	74a	Littleborough	53c
Leadenham	49d	Littlebourne	14a
Leadgate	68c	Littlehampton	11d
Leadhills	73d	Little Ouseburn	54a
Leasingham	49d	Littleport	39c
Leatherhead	18d	Littlestone-on-Sea	14c
Lechlade	16b	Little Stukeley	30b
Leconfield	56c	Little Thurlow	31b
Ledbury	27d	Liverpool	45b
Lee on the Solent	10c	Liversedge	53d
Leeds	54c	Lizard	1d
Leedstown	1d	Llanaber	33a
Leek	47c	Llanaelhaearn	43d
Leeming	61c	Llanbedr	33a
Legbourne	50a	Llanbedrog	43d
Leicester	37c	Llanberis	44a
Leigh (Grtr Manchester)	46a	Llanbrynmair	33d
Leigh on Sea	20a	Llanddewi	23c
Leighton Buzzard	30c	Llandeilo	23b
Leiston	41d	Llandinam	34c
Lendalfoot	63b	Llandissilio	22a
Leominster	27a	Llandovery	23b
Lerwick	104b	Llandrillo	44b

Llandrindod Wells	26a	Lochgilphead	78c
Llandudno	44a	Lochgoilhead	79d
Llandyssul	22b	Lochinver	97b
Llanelli	22d	Lochmaben	65b
Llanerchymedd	43b	Lochmaddy	103c
Llanfaethlu	43b	Lochranza	70a
Llanfair Caereinion	34c	Lochwinnoch	71b
Llanfairfechan	44a	Lockerbie	65b
Llanfair Talhaiarn	44b	Loddon	42c
Llanfihangel	26d	Loftus	62a
Llanfrynach	26c	Loggerheads	35b
Llanfyllin	34a	Logierait	86d
Llangadog	23b	London	19a
Llangamarch Wells	26a	London Colney	18b
Llangefni	43b	Long Bennington	37b
Llangelynin	33c	Longbenton	68c
Llangennith	22d	Long Compton	28d
Llangoed	44a	Long Crendon	17b
Llangollen	34a	Long Eaton	37a
Llangurig	33d	Longforgan	82a
Llangwnnadl	43c	Longformacus	75b
Llangybi	25b	Longframlington	68a
Llangynog	34a	Longhorsley	68a
Llanidloes	33d	Longhoughton	68a
Llanmadoc	22d	Long Newton	60b
Llanon	23a	Longniddry	82c
Llanrwst	44b	Long Preston	53a
Llansantffraid	25a	Longridge	52c
Llansawel	25d	Long Sutton (Lincs)	39a
Llansoy	15a	Long Sutton (Somerset)	8a
Llanthony	26d	Longtown	66c
Llantrisant	24c	Looe, E. & W.	3c
Llantwit Major	24c	Lossiemouth	94b
Llanuwchllyn	33b	Lostwithiel	2b
Llanwrtyd Wells	26a	Loughborough	37a
Llanybyther	25c	Louth	50a
Llanymynech	34a	Lowestoft	42c
Llanyre	26a	Lowick	76c
Llechryd	22a	Ludag	103c
Lledrod	25b	Ludgershall	17c
Llwyngwril	33a	Ludlow	27a
Llyswen	26c	Lumphanan	88a
Loanhead	74a	Lumsden	95d
Loans	71d	Luss	79d
Lochailort	84a	Luton	30d
Lochaline	84c	Lutterworth	29b
Locharbriggs	65a	Lybster	101c
Lochboisdale	103c	Lydd	14c
Lochbuie	77b	Lydford	3b
Lochcarron	90b	Lydney	15b
Lochearnhead	80a	Lyme Regis	7d
Lochgair	78c	Lyminge	14a
Lochgelly	81d	Lymington	9d

Lymm	46a
Lympne	14c
Lyndhurst	9b
Lyneham	16a
Lyness	101c
Lynmouth	6a
Lynton	6a
Lytchett Minster	9c
Lytham St.Annes	51d

M

Mablethorpe	50b
Macclesfield	46b
Macduff	95b
Machen	24d
Machrihanish	69d
Machynlleth	33c
Mackworth	36b
Macmerry	74b
Maesteg	23d
Maghull	45b
Magor	15a
Maiden Bradley	8b
Maidenhead	18a
Maiden Newton	8c
Maidens	71d
Maidstone	13b
Maldon	20a
Malham	53a
Mallaig	84a
Malmesbury	16a
Malpas	34b
Maltby	48a
Malton	55b
Malvern Wells	27d
Manchester	47a
Mangotsfield	15b
Manningtree	32d
Manorbier	21d
Mansfield	48c
Marazion	1c
March	38d
Maresfield	12a
Margam	23d
Margate	14b
Mark	15c
Market Deeping	38a
Market Drayton	35a
Market Harborough	37d
Market Rasen	49b
Market Warsop	48c
Market Weighton	55d

Markfield	37a
Markinch	82c
Marksbury	15d
Marlborough	16d
Marlow	18d
Marple	47a
Marsden (W.Yorks)	47b
Marshfield	16a
Martock	8b
Marton (Lincs)	49a
Maryculter	88b
Marykirk	88c
Maryport	57a
Masham	61c
Matlock	47d
Mauchline	72c
Maxton	75d
Maybole	71d
Mayfield	13c
Measham	36b
Meigle	87d
Meikleour	87c
Melbourn	31a
Melbourne	36b
Melksham	16c
Mellon Charles	97a
Melness	100b
Melrose	75d
Melsonby	60c
Meltham	47b
Melton Mowbray	37b
Melvaig	97a
Melvich	100d
Menai Bridge	44a
Meopham	20c
Mere	8b
Merrivale	2b
Merthyr Tydfil	24a
Messingham	49b
Methil	82c
Methlick	96c
Methven	81b
Methwold	39d
Mettingham	42c
Mevagissey	2a
Mexborough	48a
Mid Calder	74a
Middleham	60c
Middlemarsh	8a
Middlesborough	61b
Middleton (Norfolk)	39b
Middleton in Teesdale	59b
Middlewich	46c

Midgeholme	66d	Mossat	94c
Midhurst	11c	Motherwell	73b
Mid-Lavant	11c	Mountain Ash	24a
Midsomer Norton	15d	Mountsorrel	37a
Mid Yell	104b	Mousehole	1c
Mildenhall	31b	Mouswald	65d
Milford (Surrey)	11a	Mowtie	88b
Milford Haven	21d	Muchalls	88b
Millerston	72b	Much Birch	27c
Millmeece	35b	Much Hadham	31c
Millom	57d	Much Wenlock	35c
Millport	71b	Muddleswood	11d
Milnathort	81b	Muir of Fowlis	95d
Milnthorpe	51b	Muir of Ord	92a
Milovaig	89a	Muirdrum	82b
Milton	9d	Muirhead	82a
Milton Abbot	3b	Muirkirk	73c
Milton Keynes	30c	Muker	59d
Milverton	7a	Mullion	1d
Minehead	6b	Mumbles	23d
Minster (Kent, I.of Sheppey)	20d	Mumby	50d
Minster (Kent)	14a	Mundesley	40b
Minsterley	34d	Munlochy	93a
Mintlaw	96b	Murlaggan	84b
Mirfield	53d	Musselburgh	74b
Misterton (Notts)	49a	Muthill	81a
Misterton (Somerset)	8a	Mybster	101b
Mitford	68a		
Mobberley	46b	**N**	
Modbury	3d		
Moelfre	44a	Nafferton	56a
Moffat	74c	Nailsea	15d
Mold	45d	Nailsworth	16a
Moniaive	64b	Nairn	93b
Monifieth	82b	Nant-y-Moel	24c
Monkleigh	5b	Nantgarw	24c
Monks Eleigh	41a	Nantwich	46c
Monkton	72c	Narbeth	22c
Monmouth	27c	Narborough	37c
Montgomery	34c	Neath	23d
Montrose	88c	Needham Market	32b
Monyash	47d	Neilston	72a
Monymusk	95d	Nelson (Lancs)	52d
Morar	84a	Nelson (Mid Glam)	24a
Morecambe	51b	Nenthead	67d
Moresby	57a	Nenthorn	75d
Moreton in Marsh	28d	Nesscliff	34b
Moretonhampstead	4a	Neston	45b
Morley	54c	Nether Stowey	7b
Morpeth	68a	Netherwitten	68a
Morriston	23b	Nethy Bridge	94c
Mortehoe	5b	New Abbey	65c
Mortimers Cross	27a	New Aberdour	96a

Newark-on-Trent	49c	Ninfield	13c
Newbiggin-by-the-Sea	68a	Nordelph	39c
Newbigging	73b	Norham	76c
Newbridge	24b	Norman Cross	38c
Newbridge-on-Wye	26a	Normanton	54c
Newburgh	82a	Northallerton	60d
Newburgh	96d	Northampton	29b
Newburn	68c	North Bersted	11c
Newbury	17d	North Berwick	82d
Newcastle Emlyn	22a	North Cave	55d
Newcastle-under-Lyme	35b	North Elmhall	40a
Newcastle-upon-Tyne	68c	North Ferriby	55d
Newcastleton	66a	North Frodingham	56a
New Cumnock	72c	Northiam	13d
New Deer	96a	Northleach	28d
Newent	27d	North Petherton	7b
New Galloway	64a	Northolt	18b
Newhaven	12c	North Queensferry	81d
New Holland	56c	North Somercotes	50a
Newingreen	14c	North Sunderland	76d
Newlyn	1c	North Tawton	6c
Newmachar	96c	North Thoresby	50a
Newmarket	31b	North Tidworth	16d
New Mills	47a	North Tolsta	103b
Newmilns	72a	North Walsham	40b
Newnham	27d	Northwich	46c
New Pitsligo	96a	Norwich	40b
Newport (Salop)	35b	Nottingham	37a
Newport (Dyfed)	21b	Nuneaton	36d
Newport (Gwent)	15a	Nunthorpe	61b
Newport (I.o.W.)	10c	Nutley	12a
Newport Pagnell	30c		
Newport-on-Tay	82a	**O**	
New Quay	25a		
Newquay	2a	Oadby	37c
New Romney	14c	Oakham	37d
New Scone	81b	Oakhill	15d
New Seaham	68d	Oakworth	53d
Newton Abbot	4a	Oban	78a
Newton Arlosh	65d	Occumster	101a
Newton Aycliffe	60a	Ochiltree	72c
Newton Ferrers	3d	Ockley	11b
Newtongrange	75a	Ogmore	24c
Newton-le-Willows	46a	Okehampton	3b
Newton on the Moor	68a	Old Dailly	63b
Newtonmore	86a	Oldham	47a
Newton Poppleford	7c	Old Leake	50c
Newton Stewart	64c	Oldmeldrum	96c
Newtown	34c	Ollaberry	104a
Newtown St. Boswells	75d	Ollerton	48d
Newtyle	87d	Olney	30a
Neyland	21d	Onchan	51c
Nigg	93b	Ordie	87b

Orford	41c	Pencaitland	75a
Ormesby St. Margaret	42d	Penderyn	24a
Ormiston	82c	Pendine	22c
Ormskirk	45b	Penegoes	33d
Orpington	19d	Penicuik	74a
Orton	59a	Penistone	47b
Ossett	54c	Penketh	46a
Ossington	48d	Penkridge	35b
Oswaldkirk	54b	Penmaenmawr	44a
Oswaldtwistle	52c	Pennal	33c
Oswestry	34b	Penrith	58a
Otford	19d	Penryn	2c
Otley	53d	Pensford	15d
Otterbourne	10a	Penshurst	12a
Otterburn	67b	Pentraeth	44a
Otter Ferry	78c	Pentrebont	25b
Otterswick	104b	Pentre-Foelas	44d
Ottery St. Mary	7c	Penzance	1c
Oundle	38c	Perranporth	1b
Outwell	39c	Pershore	28a
Overbister	101d	Perth	81b
Overstrand	40b	Peterborough	38c
Overton (Clwyd)	34b	Peterculter	88b
Overton (Hants)	17d	Peterhead	96b
Over Whiteacre	36c	Peterlee	60b
Oxford	17b	Petersfield	10b
Oykel Bridge	97d	Petworth	11a
		Pevensey	12d
P		Pewsey	16d
		Philleigh	2c
Paddock Wood	13a	Pickering	55b
Padstow	2a	Piddletrenthide	8c
Paignton	4c	Piercebridge	61a
Painswick	16a	Pierowall	101d
Paisley	72a	Pinchbeck	38a
Pangbourne	17b	Piperspool	3a
Parkeston	32d	Pirnmill	70a
Parracombe	6a	Pitlochry	86d
Paston	40b	Pitscottie	82a
Pateley Bridge	53b	Pitsea	20a
Pathhead	74b	Pittentrail	99b
Patna	72c	Pittenweem	82d
Patrington	56a	Playden	13d
Peak Forest	47b	Plean	80d
Peasemarsh	13d	Plockton	90c
Peasenhall	41d	Pluckley	13b
Peebles	74a	Plymouth	3d
Peel	51c	Plympton	3d
Pembroke	21d	Pocklington	55b
Pembroke Dock	21d	Polbathic	3c
Pembury	13a	Polegate	12d
Penally	22c	Polmont	81d
Penarth	24d	Polperro	2b

Polzeath	2a
Ponders End	19b
Pontardawe	23b
Pontardulais	23b
Pontefract	54c
Ponteland	68c
Pontrhydfendigaid	25b
Pontyates	23a
Pontypool	15a
Pontypridd	24c
Poole	9c
Poolewe	97a
Porlock	6b
Port Appin	84d
Port Askaig	69b
Port Bannantyne	71b
Port Charlotte	69a
Port Ellen	69a
Port Erin	51c
Port Glasgow	79d
Portgower	99d
Porth	24c
Porth-y-Rhydd	22d
Porthcawl	23d
Porthleven	1d
Porthmadog	33a
Porthowen	1b
Port Isaac	2a
Portishead	15a
Portknockie	95b
Portlethen	88b
Portloe	2c
Port Logan	63c
Portmahomack	99c
Portnacroish	84d
Portnaguiran	103b
Portnahaven	69d
Port of Menteith	80a
Port of Ness	103b
Portpatrick	63c
Portree	89b
Portskerra	100c
Portsmouth	10d
Portsonachan	78b
Portsoy	95b
Port Talbot	23d
Port William	63d
Potterne	16c
Potter's Bar	19a
Potton	30b
Poulton-le-Fylde	51d
Prees	35a
Prescot	46a

Prestatyn	45a
Presteigne	26b
Preston (Lancs)	52c
Preston (Dorset)	8c
Preston Brockhurst	35a
Preston Candover	10a
Prestonpans	82b
Prestwick	71d
Princes Risborough	18a
Princetown	3b
Probus	2a
Prudhoe	68c
Puckeridge	31c
Puddletown	8d
Pudsey	53d
Pulborough	11b
Pulham	42a
Purfleet	19b
Purton	16b
Pwllheli	43d
Pycombe	12c

Q

Queenborough	20d
Queensferry	45d
Quorn	37a

R

Radcliffe (Grtr Manchester)	46b
Radcliffe on Trent	37a
Radlett	19a
Radstock	15d
Raglan	15a
Rainford	46a
Rainham	19b
Rampside	51b
Ramsbottom	52d
Ramsey (Cambs)	38d
Ramsey (I.o.M.)	51c
Ramsgate	14b
Ranby	48b
Rapness	101d
Rathen	96b
Ratlinghope	34d
Rattray	87d
Raund	30a
Ravenglass	57d
Ravenscar	62d
Rawcliffe	55c
Rawmarsh	48a
Rawtenstall	52d

Rayleigh	20a	Romanno Bridge	74a
Reading	17d	Romford	19b
Reculver	14a	Romiley	47a
Redcar	61b	Romsey	9b
Redcastle	92a	Ropley	10a
Redditch	28a	Rosehearty	96a
Redhill	12a	Rosemarkie	92b
Redruth	1d	Roskhill	89a
Reedham	42c	Roslin	74a
Reepham	42b	Ross-on-Wye	27d
Reeth	60c	Rosyth	81d
Reigate	11b	Rothbury	67b
Reiss	101b	Rotherham	48a
Rempstone	37a	Rothesay	71b
Renfrew	72a	Rothes-on-Spey	94a
Repton	36b	Rothwell (W.Yorks)	54c
Resolven	23b	Rothwell (Northants)	37d
Revesby	50c	Rottingdean	12c
Reydon	41d	Roughton	40a
Rhayader	26a	Roxton	30b
Rhiconich	98c	Royal Leamington Spa	29a
Rhondda	24a	Royal Tunbridge Wells	12b
Rhosli	22d	Roybridge	85b
Rhosneigr	43a	Royston	31c
Rhos-on-Sea	44b	Royton	47a
Rhuddan	45a	Ruabon	45d
Rhyd-Owen	25a	Rudston	56a
Rhyl	44b	Rugby	29b
Rhymney	24a	Rugeley	36a
Rhyne	95d	Runcorn	46a
Richborough	14b	Rushden	30a
Richmond	60c	Ruskington	49d
Richmond upon Thames	18d	Rutherglen	72a
Rickmansworth	18b	Ruthin	45c
Riding Mill	67d	Ruthven	87d
Ridsdale	67b	Ryde	10c
Rievaulx	61d	Rye	13d
Ringford	64c	Ryhope	68d
Ringmer	12c	Rylstone	52b
Ringwood	9d	Ryton	68c
Ripley (Derbys)	48c		
Ripley (Surrey)	11b	**S**	
Ripon	54a		
Roade	29b	Sadberge	60b
Roberton	74d	Saffron Walden	31d
Robertsbridge	13c	St.Abbs	76a
Robin Hood's Bay	62d	St.Agnes	1b
Rochdale	52d	St.Albans	18b
Rochester	13a	St.Andrews	82b
Rochford	20a	St.Asaph	45c
Rock	2a	St.Austell	2a
Rodel	103b	St.Bees	57a
Rogate	11a	St.Blazey	2b

St.Buryan	1c	Saundersfoot	22c
St.Catherines	78b	Saxilby	49d
St.Clears	22c	Saxmundham	41d
St.Columb Major	2a	Scalby	62d
St.Columb Minor	2a	Scalloway	104c
St.Combs	96b	Scamblesby	50a
St.Cyrus	88c	Scampton	49b
St.Davids	21a	Scarborough	62d
St.Devereux	27c	Scarfskerry	101b
St.Fillans	80a	Scarinish	83a
St.Germans	3c	Scartho	50a
St.Helens (Merseyside)	46a	Scleddau	21b
St.Helens (I.of W.)	10c	Sconser	89b
St.Ives (Cornwall)	1d	Scotch Corner	61c
St.Ives (Huntingdon)	31a	Scotter	49b
St.John's Chapel	59b	Scourie	98c
St.Just	1c	Scousburgh	104c
St.Keverne	2c	Scrabster	101b
St.Leonards	13d	Scriven	54a
St.Margarets at Cliffe	14b	Scrooby	48b
St.Margaret's Hope	101c	Scunthorpe	49b
St.Marys (Orkney)	101c	Seaford	12c
St.Mawes	2c	Seaham	68d
St.Mellons	24d	Seahouses	76d
St.Monans	82b	Seal	19d
St.Neots	30b	Seamer	62d
St.Ninians	81c	Seamill	71b
St.Petrox	21d	Seascale	57c
Salcombe	4c	Seaton	7d
Sale	46b	Sedbergh	58d
Salen (Highland)	84c	Sedgefield	61b
Salen (Mull)	84c	Sedgley	35d
Salford	46b	Sedlescombe	13d
Saline	81d	Seend	16c
Salisbury	9b	Selborne	10b
Saltash	3d	Selby	54d
Saltburn	62a	Selkirk	75c
Saltcoats	71b	Sellindge	14c
Saltfleet	50a	Selly Oak	36c
Sanaigmore	69a	Selsey	11c
Sandbach	46d	Selstad	14a
Sandbank	79c	Semington	16c
Sandersted	19d	Sennen	1c
Sandgate	14c	Settle	53a
Sandhead	63c	Sevenoaks	13a
Sandown	10c	Severn Stoke	28c
Sandwich	14b	Shaftesbury	8b
Sandwick	104c	Shalbourne	17c
Sandy	30b	Shalford	11b
Sannox	70b	Shanklin	10c
Sanquhar	73d	Shap	59a
Sarre	14a	Sharpness	15b
Satley	60a	Sharwell	10c

Shawbury	35a	Slapton	4c
Sheerness	20b	Sleaford	49d
Sheffield	48a	Sledmere	55b
Shefford	30d	Sleights	62c
Shepton Mallet	8a	Slough	18a
Sherborne	8a	Slyne	51b
Sherburn in Elmet	54c	Smailholm	75d
Shere	11b	Smithfield	66c
Sheringham	40a	Smithwick	36c
Sherston	16a	Smoo	98d
Shieldaig	90a	Snaith	55c
Shifnal	35d	Snodland	13a
Shildon	60a	Soham	31b
Shillingford	17b	Solihull	28b
Shilton	36d	Solva	21a
Shipley	53d	Somerton	8a
Shipston on Stour	28d	Sompting	11d
Shipton-under-Wychwood	28d	Sonning	18c
Shoeburyness	20b	Sorn	72c
Shoreham by Sea	11d	Soulby	58b
Shotley	41a	Sourton	3b
Shotley Bridge	68c	Southall	18b
Shotton	45d	Southam	29a
Shotts	73b	Southampton	9b
Shrewsbury	34b	South Brent	4c
Shrivenham	17a	Southend-on-Sea	20a
Sidcot	15c	Southery	39c
Sidcup	19d	South Ferriby	55d
Siddington	46d	South Harting	10b
Sidford	7d	South Hayling	10d
Sidlesham	10d	South Kelsey	49b
Sidmouth	7c	South Kilvington	61d
Silkstone	47b	South Mimms	19a
Silloth	65d	Southminster	20b
Silsden	53b	South Molton	6a
Silverdale	51b	South Ockendon	19b
Silverstone	29d	South Otterington	61d
Simonburn	67d	South Petherton	7b
Simonsbath	6b	Southport	51d
Singleton	11c	South Queensferry	81d
Sissinghurst	13d	Southsea	10c
Sittingbourne	13b	South Shields	68d
Sixpenny Handley	9a	Southwell	48d
Skaill	101c	Southwold	41d
Skegness	50d	Sowerby Bridge	53d
Skelmersdale	46a	Spalding	38b
Skelmorlie	71b	Sparkford	8a
Skelton	61b	Spean Bridge	85a
Skewen	23b	Spennymoor	60a
Skipsea	56a	Spetchley	28a
Skipton	52d	Spey Bay	94b
Slaidburn	52a	Spilsby	50c
Slammanan	81c	Spinningdale	99a

Spittal	76a	Stoke-on-Trent	35b
Spittal of Glenshee	87c	Stokenchurch	18a
Spofforth	54a	Stokesay	27a
Springholm	64b	Stokesley	61d
Sproatley	56c	Stone (Staffs)	35b
Sprouston	75d	Stone (Glos)	15b
Stadhampton	17b	Stonehaven	88b
Staffin	89b	Stonehouse	16a
Stafford	35b	Stoneykirk	63c
Stagsden	30a	Stonor	18a
Staindrop	60a	Stony Stratford	29d
Staines	18d	Stornoway	103b
Staithes	62a	Storrington	11d
Stalbridge	8b	Stourbridge	28a
Stalybridge	47a	Stourport	27b
Stamford	38c	Stow (Borders)	75c
Stamford Bridge	54b	Stow on the Wold	28d
Standish	46a	Stowmarket	32a
Stanford le Hope	20c	Strachan	88a
Stanhope	59b	Stradsett	39d
Stanley (Durham)	68c	Stranraer	63c
Stanley (Tayside)	81b	Stratford St.Mary	32d
Stanlow	45b	Stratford-upon-Avon	28b
Stanmore	18b	Strathaven	72b
Stannington	68a	Strathcanaird	97c
Stanstead Abbots	19b	Strathmiglo	81b
Stansted	31d	Strathpeffer	92a
Stapleford	37a	Strathy	100d
Staplehurst	13b	Strathyre	80a
Starcross	4b	Stratton	5d
Staveley (Cumbria)	58c	Streatley	17b
Staveley (Derbys)	48c	Street	8a
Staxton	56a	Strensall	55a
Stein	89a	Stretford	46b
Stenhousemuir	80d	Strichen	96a
Stepps	73a	Stromeferry	90d
Stevenage	30d	Stromness	101d
Stevenston	71b	Stronachlachar	79b
Stewarton	72a	Stronmilchan	79b
Steyning	11d	Strontian	84c
Stibb Cross	5d	Stroud	16a
Stickney	50c	Struan	86c
Stiffkey	40a	Struy	92c
Stillington	54b	Studland	9c
Stilton	38c	Studley	28a
Stirling	80d	Sturminster Newton	8b
Stithians	1d	Sturry	14a
Stock	20a	Sturton	49b
Stockbridge	9b	Sudbury	32c
Stockport	46b	Sumburgh	104c
Stocksbridge	47b	Summer Bridge	53b
Stockton-on-Tees	60b	Sunderland	68d
Stoke Mandeville	18a	Surbiton	18d

Sutton	**19c**	Terrington St.Clement	**39a**
Sutton Benger	**16a**	Tetbury	**16a**
Sutton Bridge	**39a**	Tewkesbury	**28c**
Sutton Coldfield	**36c**	Thame	**17b**
Sutton in Ashfield	**48c**	Thamesmead	**19b**
Sutton on Sea	**50b**	Thatcham	**17d**
Swadlincote	**36b**	Thetford	**32a**
Swainsthorpe	**42a**	The Witterings	**10d**
Swanage	**9c**	Thirsk	**54a**
Swansea	**23d**	Thornaby-on-Tees	**60b**
Swindon	**16b**	Thornbury	**15b**
Swineshead	**38a**	Thorne	**55c**
Swinton (Grtr Manchester)	**46b**	Thornhill	**64b**
Swinton (Borders)	**76a**	Thornton	**82c**
Symington	**73d**	Thornton Curtis	**56c**
Symonds Yat	**27d**	Thornton Dale	**62c**
Syston	**37a**	Thorpeness	**41d**
		Thrapston	**30a**
T		Thropton	**67b**
		Thursby	**65d**
Tadcaster	**54c**	Thurso	**101a**
Tadley	**17d**	Ticehurst	**13c**
Tain	**99c**	Tichfield	**10c**
Talerddig	**33d**	Tickhill	**48a**
Talley	**23b**	Tighnabruach	**78d**
Talybont	**33c**	Tilbury	**20c**
Tamworth	**36c**	Tillicoultry	**81c**
Tannadice	**87d**	Timberscombe	**6b**
Tarbert (W.Isles)	**103a**	Tintagel	**5c**
Tarbert (Strathclyde)	**70a**	Tintern	**15a**
Tarbolton	**72c**	Tiptree	**22c**
Tarporley	**46c**	Tipton	**35d**
Tarrant Hinton	**9a**	Tiverton	**7a**
Tarskavaig	**84a**	Tobermory	**83d**
Tarves	**96c**	Toddington	**30c**
Tarvin	**46c**	Todhills	**87d**
Tattershall	**50c**	Todmorden	**53c**
Taunton	**7b**	Tolleshunt D'Arcy	**20b**
Tavistock	**3b**	Tolob	**104c**
Taynuilt	**78b**	Tomatin	**93d**
Tayport	**82a**	Tomintoul	**94c**
Tayvallich	**78c**	Tomnavoulin	**94c**
Teangue	**90c**	Tonbridge	**13a**
Tedburn St.Mary	**4a**	Tongland	**64d**
Teignmouth	**4a**	Tongue	**100b**
Telford	**35a**	Tonyrefail	**24c**
Templand	**65b**	Topcliffe	**54a**
Templecombe	**8a**	Topsham	**4b**
Temple Ewell	**14b**	Torcross	**4c**
Tenbury Wells	**27b**	Torgyle	**91d**
Tenby	**22c**	Torksey	**49a**
Tenterden	**13d**	Torpoint	**3d**
Terrington	**54b**	Torquay	**4c**

Torridon	90b
Torryburn	81d
Torver	57d
Toscaig	90c
Totland	9d
Totnes	4c
Totton	9b
Towcester	29b
Tow Law	60a
Tranent	74b
Trantlebeg	100c
Traquair	74d
Trawsfynydd	33a
Tredegar	24b
Tredington	28d
Treen	1c
Trefriw	44a
Tregaron	25b
Tregony	2c
Trelech	22a
Tremadog	44c
Tresla	104a
Tricketts Cross	9c
Trimdon	60b
Tring	18a
Trochry	86d
Troed-y-thiw	24a
Troon	71d
Trowbridge	16c
Trowse Newton	42a
Trumpington	31a
Truro	2a
Tufton	21b
Tullibody	80d
Tumble	22d
Turnberry	71d
Turrif	96a
Tutbury	36a
Tuxford	48d
Twickenham	18d
Twycross	36d
Twyford (Berks)	18a
Twyford (Hants)	10a
Twyn-Llanan	23b
Twynholm	64c
Tydd St.Mary	38b
Tywyn	33c

U

Uckfield	12a
Ufford	41b
Uig	89b
Ulceby	56c
Ullapool	97a
Ulpha	57d
Ulverston	51b
Umberleigh	6a
Upavon	16d
Upminster	19b
Upper Broughton	37b
Uppingham	37d
Upstreet	14a
Upton	28c
Urchfont	16c
Urmston	46b
Usk	15a
Uttoxeter	36a
Uxbridge	18b
Uyeasound	104b

V

Vange	20a
Ventnor	10c
Verwood	9a
Voe	104a

W

Waddington (Lancs)	52a
Waddington (Lincs)	49d
Wadebridge	2a
Wadhurst	13c
Wainfleet	50d
Wakefield	54c
Wakes Colne	32c
Walberswick	41d
Walkerburn	74d
Wallasey	45b
Wallingford	17b
Walls	104a
Wallsend	68d
Walmer	14b
Walpole	41d
Walsall	36c
Walsingham	40a
Waltham	50a
Waltham Abbey	19b
Waltham Cross	19a
Walton-on-the-Naze	32d
Wantage	17a
Warboys	38d
Warcop	59b
Wardington	29a
Ware	31c

Wareham	9c	Westgate on Sea	14b
Wargrave	18a	Westhoughton	46a
Warley	36c	West Kilbride	71b
Warlingham	19c	West Lavington	16c
Warmington	29a	West Linton	74a
Warminster	16c	West Lulworth	8c
Warning	13c	West Malling	20c
Warrington	46a	West Meon	10a
Warslow	47d	West Mersea	32c
Warter	55b	Westmeston	12c
Warton	51d	West Moors	9c
Warwick	28b	Weston (Staffs)	35b
Washford	7a	Weston on the Green	29d
Washington	68c	Weston-super-Mare	15c
Watchet	7a	West Runton	40a
Waterlooville	10a	West Witton	60c
Watford	18b	Wetheral	66c
Wath Brow	57a	Wetherby	54a
Wath-upon-Dearne	48a	Weybourne	40a
Watlington	17b	Weybridge	18d
Watten	101b	Weymouth	8c
Watton	39d	Whaleybridge	47a
Watton	42a	Whalley	52c
Wear Head	59b	Wharram-le-Street	55b
Weaverham	46c	Whickham	68c
Weaverthorpe	55b	Whiddon Down	6c
Wedmore	15c	Whiltingham	76c
Weedon Bec	29b	Whipsnade	30c
Weeford	36c	Whitbeck	57d
Weem	86c	Whitburn	68d
Weeting	39d	Whitby	62a
Wellingborough	30a	Whitchurch (Hants)	17d
Wellington (Somerset)	7a	Whitchurch (Salop)	35a
Wellington (Salop)	35a	Whitehall	101d
Wells (Somerset)	15d	Whitehaven	57a
Wells (Norfolk)	39b	Whitehills	95b
Welshampton	34b	Whithorn	64c
Welshpool	34a	Whiting Bay	70d
Welwyn Garden City	19a	Whitland	22c
Wem	35a	Whitley Bay	68d
Wemyss Bay	71b	Whitney	17a
Wendens Ambo	31d	Whitstable	14a
Wendlebury	29d	Whitstone	5d
Wendover	18a	Whittington	58c
Wentbridge	54c	Whittlesey	38d
West Auckland	61a	Whitton Gilbert	68c
West Bridgford	37a	Whittonstall	58c
West Bromwich	36c	Wibsey	53d
West Burton	59d	Wick	101a
Westbury	16c	Wickford	20a
West Calder	73b	Wickham	10a
West Coker	8a	Wickham Market	41b
Westerham	19d	Wickwar	15b

Widecombe	4a	Woodbridge	41a
Widnes	46a	Woodchurch	13d
Wigan	46a	Woodford	19b
Wigston	37c	Woodhall Spa	50c
Wigton	65d	Woodstock	29c
Wigtown	64c	Woodyates	9a
Wilby	41b	Woofferton	27a
Willingdon	12d	Wool	8d
Willingham	31a	Woolacombe	5b
Willington	60a	Wooler	76c
Williton	7a	Woolwich	19b
Wilmslow	46b	Wooton Basset	16b
Wilsontown	73b	Worbrough	48a
Wilton	9a	Worcester	28a
Wimborne Minster	9c	Workington	57a
Wincanton	8a	Worksop	48a
Winchcombe	28c	Worle	15c
Winchelsea	13d	Wormit	82a
Winchester	10a	Worthen	34d
Windermere	58c	Worthing	11d
Windsor	18c	Wotton under Edge	16a
Wingham	14a	Wragby	49b
Winkfield	18c	Wrangle	50c
Winkleigh	6c	Wrexham	45d
Winsford	46c	Writtle	20a
Winslow	29d	Wrotham Heath	20c
Winster	57c	Wroxham	42b
Winterbourne (Avon)	15b	Wybunbury	46c
Winterbourne Abbas	8c	Wych Cross	12a
Winterbourne Stoke	9a	Wylye	9a
Winteringham	55d	Wymondham	42a
Wirksworth	47d		
Wisbech	38d	**Y**	
Wisborough Green	11b		
Wishaw	73b	Yarcombe	7b
Witham	32c	Yardley Gobion	29d
Witheridge	6d	Yarm	60b
Withernsea	56d	Yarmouth	9d
Withington	46b	Yatton	15c
Withleigh	6d	Yaxley	38c
Wittersham	13d	Yeadon	53d
Witton-le-Wear	60a	Yealmpton	3d
Wiveliscombe	7a	Yelverton	3b
Wivenhoe	32c	Yeovil	8a
Woking	18d	Yetholm	76c
Wokingham	18c	Yetts of Muckart	81
Wollaston	30a	York	54
Wolsingham	60a	Youlgreave	47
Wolverhampton	35d	Ysbyty Ystwyth	2
Wolverton	17d	Ystalyfera	2
Wombwell	48a	Ystradgynlais	2